The Sensitive Person's Survival Guide

An Alternative Health Answer to Emotional Sensitivity & Depression

Kyra Mesich, Psy.D.

A▧▧▧▧   P▧ ▧▧▧

The Sensitive Person's Survival Guide
An Alternative Health Answer to Emotional Sensitivity & Depression

Contact the author, Dr. Kyra Mesich at
www.KyraMesich.com

Ansuz Press
PO Box 80208
Minneapolis, MN 55408

Disclaimer:

All case examples and stories mentioned in this book are true. Some of the case
examples are based on composites of clients, whereas others are the story of
one individual. In all cases, names and identifying information have been
changed to protect confidentiality.
The information in this book is not intended as a substitute for care from
qualified practitioners.

ISBN: 0-9674767-9-8

Printed in the United States of America

This book is dedicated to all those sensitive people who have the courage to search for the true cause of their suffering.

The Sensitive Person's Survival Guide

Y

K Kyra M, Psy. D.

Other Works By Dr. Kyra Mesich

Hyperactive: Alternative Therapies for Attention-Deficit Children and Their Tired Parents

Modern Meditation: Increase Your Physical & Emotional Well-Being with a Fun, Effective Approach to Meditation

Quit Smoking: Alternative Health Solutions

These e-book titles and many more are available through Dr. Mesich's website at:

www.KyraMesich.com

Contents

Foreword
By Carol L. Philpot, Psy.D.

In the early days of its existence, the practice and study of clinical psychology, like medicine, was part science, part art. In the last half century, the scientific portion of psychology has been highly emphasized due to the Zeitgeist of a modern society that assigns greater respect to scientific inquiry than to artistic endeavors. Currently, in both psychology and medicine, the pendulum is swinging back toward holistic medicine, that is, treating the whole individual, including those portions that defy scientific explanation, such as the soul.

In *The Sensitive Person's Survival Guide*, Dr. Mesich discusses an alternative explanation for chronic depression and offers self-help techniques to alleviate the symptoms. Dr. Mesich hypothesizes that although all people have the capacity to feel the pain of another through psychic abilities, in today's society some individuals lose that skill due to socialization in a world that denies the existence of psychic phenomena. She believes that in many cases, though, people do not lose that ability. In those cases, depression may be a result of sustained bombardment with emotions emanating from others, accompanied by an inability to understand that those emotions come from outside oneself. In this book, she tells the compelling stories of several individuals for whom this appeared to be the case, including herself. Using her personal experience as a guide, she supplies the reader with methods to harness the power of psychic empathy, rather than being controlled by it. Her suggestions lead to three positive outcomes—the sensitive individual (1) is no longer overcome by depression, (2) is empowered to use psychic abilities in decision-making, and (3) can work with others more effectively.

In a time when psychology as a science has failed to adequately address the needs of complex human beings, alternative explanations such as those in this book are welcomed. *The Sensitive Person's Survival Guide* may not be grounded in traditional psychological theory and research, but it stimulates thinking and opens new possibilities. I think you will find it compelling.

-Carol L. Philpot, Psy.D.
Dean, School of Psychology, Florida Institute of Technology
Author of *Bridging Separate Gender Worlds*

Epigraph

People suffer in countless ways from their sensitivity, depression being the most common, and most are never properly diagnosed, only medicated. Reading *The Sensitive Person's Survival Guide* gave me a ray of hope that the day is coming when the maladies of empathic people will be taken seriously and treated in a more realistic way.

I couldn't help but think of the hundreds of clients and students I've worked with over the years who would greatly benefit from the wisdom written in these pages. Thank you Dr. Mesich for taking the time to write this very valuable book.

-Echo Bodine, author of *Echoes of the Soul*

Acknowledgements

Thanks to Lora Alexander for her skillful editing.

I appreciate the support and encouragement I received from all my family and friends over the many, many months it took to complete this project.

Eternal thanks goes to my husband, Michael. Without his loving patience, this book would not exist.

Chapter 1

The Transformation of a Psychologist

While working as a psychologist several years ago, I had an experience that challenged the very core of my understanding of emotions. I had received years of training in psychological theory. I had an understanding of the reasons behind people's emotions and psychological symptoms. Relatively early in my career I had already seen so much trauma, emotional pain, depression, despair and the full gamut of psychological disorders that I thought there was nothing that would ever surprise me. I was wrong. I was not prepared for an emotional incident that had no logical explanation. It had never been covered in a single textbook or seminar. I had no foundation, no theory, and no framework to use as I sat in my office confronted with a psychological situation like no other.

In order for me to explain exactly what this situation was, it is necessary to tell you the events that lead up to it.

Part I: Inexplicable Depression

It was 8:00 pm on a Monday evening, and I was cleaning up the dishes from dinner. We had a good pasta dinner that night, so we were full and satisfied. I proceeded to rinse the dishes in the sink while my husband went over to the computer in the next room to work. While I did the mindless chores in the kitchen, I thought about what I wanted to do for the rest of the evening. I always had a few partially read books lying around. Maybe I could change into my pajamas and curl up with one of those. I figured I wouldn't be staying up too late. Work had tired me out today.

I worked in a large counseling center as a psychologist. Today, like most days, my schedule had been completely full. In some ways I was still getting used to this job. We moved so I could accept this position after receiving my doctoral degree in clinical psychology. It was taking us months to adjust. It was a good job for me, but it was a lot of work. I was usually exhausted by the end of the day, so I was lucky that most evenings I could make time to rest and relax before going to bed. That was my plan for tonight as well.

My mind drifted in and out of thought while I finished the last of the dishes. Then suddenly my mood changed. I was overtaken by a wash of sickening depression that seemed to come out of nowhere. My heart sank as I took in a deep sigh. A dark abyss had opened, and I was promptly falling in. This dark depression came on so suddenly it took me aback. I was perplexed as to why it would come on out of the blue.

The depression raged on throughout the evening despite my efforts to intellectually analyze it. I changed my approach to distraction. Maybe if I read. No, I couldn't concentrate. Depressing thoughts circled over and over in my mind. Maybe if I put on some music. I tried to do some light exercise while I listened to a CD, but that activity soon deteriorated. I stopped and noticed that the song that was playing was a sad ballad of love gone wrong. It was not helping me feel any better. It felt like that song was driving right into me. Not the words, really, but the sad melody resonated perfectly with the depression I was feeling. The resonance seemed to pull me down even further. I turned it off and retreated to the bedroom in tears.

Besides feeling horribly sad and empty, depressing thoughts churned repeatedly in my head. I couldn't stop them no matter what I tried. "I am a failure. There is no hope for my future. I've screwed up my life. Things will never change." These were the mantras that wouldn't go away. I was extremely frustrated. Where did this depression come from? I knew all the things to do to lessen a depressive episode, and none of them had made a dent in this one. I was trapped in a dark hole, and I had no idea why.

I climbed into bed and angrily scrawled in my journal, "Why is this happening? I'm so depressed. Why do I feel so much pain? Thoughts are going over and over in my head about failure and hopelessness. It's strange. Why would I be thinking that now? I've never thought that before. It's not logical. It doesn't make any sense. I want this horrible feeling to go away. I'm tired of being depressed. Please let me feel better in the morning. I can't stand this." Utterly exhausted and defeated, I fell hard asleep.

The next thing I was aware of was the jarring sound of my alarm clock the next morning. I got up and went through my normal routine; brush the teeth, breakfast, some stretching. I was still reeling from the night before. I felt odd, but thankfully, not as abjectly depressed. Since I was feeling better, there was no reason not to go to work. I got in my car and departed on my usual route to work, not realizing what the day would hold.

My workdays always began with retrieving my schedule from the secretary. Since I was still feeling off kilter, I hoped I wouldn't have a full schedule of clients today. But, of course, that was not the case. I was booked solid. I even had an extra client, Dan, request to be fit in. The only time the secretary could find for him was right in the middle of the day, infringing on my lunchtime. Dan had a habit of canceling or rescheduling his appointments, so I wondered if he would really show up today. My first client showed up promptly, so I didn't have a chance to give Dan another thought.

I saw one patient after another until afternoon, when I retreated into the break room for something to eat. All too soon, the secretary found me to let me know that Dan had arrived. I walked back through the waiting room and gave Dan a nod of acknowledgement to let him know I would be right with him. I grabbed his file to remind myself of the issues we had been working on.

Dan was the epitome of nice guys finish last. Skinny and unsure of himself, he had a good heart, but very low self esteem. He had suffered from depression on and off for many years. His main issues were loneliness and worries about job failures. Most of the times I saw him, he was feeling ambivalent, not sure how to proceed with his life to change things for the better. But today when he walked into my office, he looked particularly grim.

Dan quickly announced that he had an especially painful depressive episode last night. That is why he called and asked the secretary to fit him in today. He forcefully handed me a piece of paper, which he said was a poem he had written. He thought it expressed his painful emotions well, so I should read it. As a dutiful young psychologist does, I took out my notepad and asked Dan to take a breath, slow down, and tell me more about the events of last evening. Dan had seen psychotherapists on and off for many years, so he was well prepared for this question. He began describing what happened during his depressive episode, divulging his feelings and behaviors in every detail. His depression had been set off by a rebuff from a woman he had been enamored with.

Dan had been depressed many times before in his life, but this was one of the most intense episodes he had ever had. He felt trapped and overcome by such horrible, deep depression this time that it scared him. He couldn't bring himself out of it no matter what he tried. Terribly depressing thoughts churned over and over in his mind. I asked Dan what those thoughts were. "I am a complete failure. I've screwed up my life beyond repair. I have no hope for my future. Things will never change," was his reply.

I put down the notepad and focused my attention on Dan's words. I was beginning to realize something inconceivable. "What prompted you to write this poem?" I inquired. Dan quickly replied, "I was listening to my new Indigo Girls CD. There is a song on there that is so sad. I felt like it could have been the story of me. It inspired me to write down words of my own pain. So late into the night I listened to that song and worked on that poem."

I hoped Dan didn't notice my mouth fall open in shock. I felt like a ton of bricks had just been dropped on top of me. I was baffled and dismayed. Dan had just described in perfect detail, every single facet of the depression I had felt last night. It was uncanny. The intense quality of the emotional pain, the exact thoughts, the precise time the depression began, and now I found out that we had been listening to the same CD. The song that drove into me like a knife was the very song that inspired Dan to write his poem. I was taken aback.

Dan probably felt like I was the most attentive therapist in the world that day. I focused intently on his words, searching for anything that would make our simultaneous depressions a coincidence. My head felt like a fog. His words echoed like we were in a canyon, while my thoughts raced. This isn't possible. How could this happen? But his descriptions continued to make it more and more obvious. I had literally felt Dan's emotions, at the same time he was experiencing them. It was far beyond coincidence. Every detail of the experience of our depressive episodes was the same.

After Dan left my office, I closed the door solidly behind me and plopped down hard in my chair. I needed to analyze what had just happened. Dan had described in perfect detail the exact mood, thoughts and circumstances of the depression I experienced last night. I was horrified. But I had to admit that one small part of me was relieved to have an explanation. I couldn't understand why I had suddenly, out of nowhere, felt such intense depression. The depressing thoughts I had about failure and hopelessness didn't make any sense to me. They were not the kind of thoughts I would have, even if I was depressed. Finding out that the song that was so painful I had to turn it off was the very song that Dan was listening to repeatedly...Well, it drove the point home. I couldn't shrug this off as a coincidence. It was strange, seemingly unexplainable, but that did not mean it didn't happen. I had to accept the reality of it. The deeply painful depression I went through last night was not my own at all. It was Dan's.

I made it through the rest of the day, leaving for home the first moment it was possible. I had to tell my husband. I needed his help to sort this all out. Fortunately, my husband is a very open-minded and supportive person who did not judge my story. He accepted it the same as I did, as an event that had occurred despite being inexplicable. He also was somewhat relieved that there was an explanation for the terrible depression that overcame me last night. But he also knew that this was an overwhelming and scary thing for me.

I thought more about it over the next few days. I realized right away that if Dan had not come in for an appointment that day, I would never have known that it was his emotions I was feeling. Even if he had come in a few days later, his description would not have been so vivid, and my experience of the depression would have faded. I probably would not have made the connection. I found this concept frightening. Had I felt other patient's emotions in the past and not realized it? I was afraid it would happen again. If it did, how would I be able to know? When I felt Dan's depression, it was very much like it was my own emotions. Although it was an unusual type of depression for me, I would not have had any reason to think it was anything but my own emotions if I hadn't seen Dan the next day. I was alarmed and angered by this emotional event. "Great," I thought, "I have enough problem dealing with my own emotions. Now I have to feel other people's emotions too?" I sincerely hoped not. I decided to stop pondering it further. Maybe it would never happen again. With any luck, this was just a one-time fluke occurrence.

Right. Not even a couple weeks had passed before it happened again. But this time, it wasn't Dan's emotions I felt. In fact, I never felt Dan's emotions again. Each time it happened, it was from a different client. The next occurrence happened when I felt my heart race, anxiety, and tension throughout my body while I was out walking. It turned out to be the experience of one of my female clients who had panic attacks when she had to drive over a bridge. Not much later I was overwhelmed again by feelings of depression, but this time with an undertone of mistrust and disdain for others. My experience was described by a client I was seeing who had been traumatized by a robbery.

Over the next several months I lost count of the number of times I felt the emotions of one of my patients. Each time I would feel an intense and distinct wave of painful emotions as if it was my own feelings. I wouldn't know for sure if it was my own feelings or someone else's until I would see the client later who perfectly described the strong emotions I felt. This happened with clients of all different types, male and female. The only commonality was that they were all clients I had seen more than once.

I was overwhelmed, scared and angry that this was happening to me. One day I came home in tears and pleaded to my husband to help me figure out what to do. I couldn't take it anymore. It was as if my work had completely taken over my life. My clients might as well have burst through my front door, sat down in the middle of the living room and proceeded to cry and tell sad tales of their pain and woe all through the night. I felt their emotions beyond my control. My personal life was no respite from the painful emotions a psychologist works with everyday. I was especially angered because it had always been important to me to distinctly separate my personal from my professional life. I didn't see clients outside of sessions. I maintained professional boundaries, but those boundaries obviously didn't have any influence over the emotions that I somehow sensed outside of my conscious control.

I can't imagine what it was like for my husband to see me suffer through this. I was mystified and overwhelmed. I hated that this was happening to me. I wanted nothing to do with it. Feeling these foreign, painful emotions over and over was wearing me down. I was fatigued and overwrought. There was nowhere for me to turn for help. I hid my experiences from my coworkers. I could just imagine the expressions on their faces if I had told them. By conventional psychological standards, my experience would fall under the label of psychosis. My fellow therapists would have said I was delusional, and that it is absolutely not possible to feel another person's emotions. I didn't have the strength to defend my experiences to them. It was best to keep it under wraps. Hopefully, my husband and I would soon figure out what was happening to me, and what I could do about it.

Unfortunately, we didn't turn up much in our initial research. We obtained new books and read about various types of psychic phenomena. Nothing seemed to describe my experiences exactly. All we could figure out was that somehow I was sensing my clients' intense emotions. Based on some of these readings, I started a regular routine of meditation during which I visualized being shielded and protected from these outside emotions. I felt like this was a good start, but it didn't have much effect. I was still vulnerable to feeling other's emotions, although it happened a little less often. To top it off, I was beginning to become aware that I was also sensing the emotions of friends, as well as clients.

I was thoroughly exhausted and drained. It didn't seem like there was any way to make this stop happening. I was overwrought with confusion about my career. How could I work as a psychologist in the years to come if this never stopped? Back in college when I had to make a career choice, I had been internally compelled to psychology. I knew it was the direction I should go. Now I wondered why. I had grave doubts about my ability to function as a psychotherapist for much longer. After 8 years of college and a promising first few years, this was not a thought I entertained lightly. But I couldn't keep working like this much longer. How could I even explain to anybody what was happening? All that time and money invested into a career that was doing me in. Things looked bleak. As if this weren't enough, I developed severe pain in one of my legs. I was diagnosed with blood clots and admitted to the hospital. It was a dreadful experience, but at least I was able to rest for a while.

Soon afterward my husband received a job offer in another state. There was no hesitation in his acceptance. We both knew it would be best for me to leave this workplace behind. In the time I worked at the counseling center, I saw many of my clients make good progress. I did not directly experience the emotions of most of my patients. But, beginning with Dan, there were those clients whose emotions I experienced as if they were my own feelings. It was as if two worlds collided in my office. The world of the rational therapist who charted clients' progress, pointed out the origins of behaviors, and broke their suffering down into logical, understandable components was shattered by an unexplainable event. There were no more boundaries, no safe place, no professional, intellectual distance. There was only the raw, pure energy of emotional pain and trauma. And there was no escaping it.

Part II: Empathy

As we settled into our new home, things started to seem a little more promising. I felt rested after a couple months off. We liked our new town, and my husband was happy with his job. Maybe things would be all right after all. We needed two incomes, so I had to start thinking about finding a job. I began to kid myself that maybe my inexplicable emotional experiences wouldn't happen again. I began looking for a new psychology position. As the prospects became more real and interviews loomed, I hesitated. What if it happens again? I was terribly conflicted. From a professional standpoint I needed to find a new job that was commensurate with my degree. A gap on my resume so early in my career would be devastating. It would greatly impact my ability to find a job later. Yet my gut was gnawing at me. I knew a door had been opened that couldn't be shut. I was lying to myself if I thought it wouldn't happen again. A couple months of rest wouldn't be the ultimate solution. I wasn't prepared to go through the same experiences again.

Eventually, I decided to look for employment in other areas, and obtained a position running an art gallery. In some ways it seemed like the perfect job for me. I hoped it would be a calm, restful place that would afford me time to recuperate. The only real stress was dodging questions from friends and family about what the heck I was doing. Why wasn't I working in a psychology job? They were puzzled. I'm sure my replies seemed empty. I was still unwilling to tell anybody about my strange emotional incidents. With no name for the experiences nor any understanding of how they happened, it was too difficult to try to explain. Internally, I was feeling ashamed and guilty that I wasn't the psychologist I had planned to be. I needed to research and understand what had happened to me. I had to find out the reason for these emotional experiences that caused me to put my career on hold.

This time my research was much more fruitful. I found out that my experiences did indeed have a name – empathic ability. Empathy is the ability to literally feel someone else's emotions as if they were your own feelings. Some modern writers call it psychic feeling. Now I at least had a name for it. I found out that empathy is actually quite common. It is the most common psychic ability. Well, step one down, a ton more to go. I still needed to know how to control empathy. Could I manage it so that it didn't occur so haphazardly? Could I tone it down so that I didn't experience such pain associated with it? I was finding more information than I had before, so I felt like I was moving forward.

In retrospect, I realize that I accomplished a lot during this time period because I could study my empathic ability from a little more distance. With my gallery job, I was not exposed to intense emotions like the jobs I was used to. It was like a vacation. Plus, since we had moved to a new state and knew hardly anyone, I had few connections with people. I was free to study empathy without it constantly bombarding me. With such a long respite, I almost began to think I had it under control.

My husband and I enjoy working in community theatre, so we got involved in a local production where we met Gary. Gary was a bright-eyed, handsome, middle-aged man who was a musician. To look at him you wouldn't know there was anything wrong. But as soon as he opened his mouth, it became obvious that he was not satisfied with his life. He hoped for fame and fortune in his musical career, but had come nowhere close. He also was very lonely. He had a long string of failed relationships. In some ways, he reminded me of Dan. That should have been a tip-off, but it wasn't. Gary liked to be around us, so we occasionally had him over. We found out that the house we were planning to purchase was near where Gary lived. It seemed like we would be pals after all.

The purchase of our new house became official, and my life became extremely busy. Sorting, packing, and preparing for the move were foremost on my mind. It also happened that I had a family gathering I needed to fly home for, so I was trying to get as much preparation done as possible before I had to leave for a few days. That's why I was surprised when I woke up the next morning feeling completely apathetic. I could barely motivate myself to get out of bed, much less start in on the chores I had planned for the day. I had so much to do, I drug myself out of bed and forced myself to do something. I was puzzled by this apathy. I was very excited about our new house, and I was eager to move. I hardly ever felt apathetic, yet I was sitting there like a lump of lead, with no motivation to do anything. I had to do my best to shrug it off. I had a hundred things to accomplish. There was no time for this.

That evening my husband and I were at our new house fixing up a few things in preparation for our move. Since Gary lived so nearby, he stopped by to see the new place. We took a break and sat out on the back porch. Unfortunately, Gary was not in a good mood that night. He had a failed date, which launched him into a diatribe about his loneliness. My husband and I listened, trying to figure out when we could change the subject. Then Gary said something that caught my attention, "I've been completely apathetic for the past few days. I don't get anything done. I can hardly motivate myself to get out of bed in the mornings."

The source of my apathy had been identified. I was irritated. I wasn't working as a psychologist anymore, but here it was happening again. I took it as a sign that I definitely did not have this empathic ability under control. There still was much more I needed to learn. In the meantime, to protect myself from Gary's emotions, I decided to cut off contact with him. It wasn't difficult to do with this particular relationship, but I realized that it wouldn't always be an option. I had to find other means to protect myself from painful empathic emotions.

I had always been interested in alternative health. I had previously studied herbs and aromatherapy, so it was natural for me to look to alternative health remedies for help in managing my empathy. I was relieved to find that flower essences appeared to hold the key. Flower essences are used for healing emotions, and many different kinds of essences relate to empathic sorts of issues. But which ones applied the most? I would have to experiment and see. Now that I didn't feel such animosity toward my empathy, I could think more objectively and deeply about it. I had to admit that I was an empathic person, and always would be. Conversely, did that also mean that I always had been? I reasoned that it was not at all likely that my empathic ability suddenly began while I was working at the counseling center. Empathy seemed more like a personality trait, like a characteristic that a person is born with.

I followed this train of thought to try to make sense of things. At the counseling center, I only realized I had empathically felt Dan's emotions because he described them so completely. There was no way I could dismiss it as coincidence. Working as a psychologist allowed me to verify that the emotions I had felt were not my own. For the first time, I was grateful that I had been working as a psychologist. In what other type of relationship can you get such detailed, accurate information about another person's emotional experience? In other types of relationships, such as with friends, family, or coworkers, these people generally hide their painful feelings. At best you see an incomplete picture of just the emotions you happen to witness or they choose to share. In these types of relationships how could an empathic person ever know for sure whether what she was feeling was coming from someone else? This made me think about my own past struggles with recurrent depression. Could it have been caused by empathy all along?

Part III: The Solution to a Lifetime of Emotional Pain

I had suffered from depression my entire life, even as a young child. It was the bane of my existence. At least a few times a year I would succumb to severe, sometimes suicidal depression. The depression recurred no matter what I did, no matter what was going on in my life. I had tried everything to get rid of it. I went through psychotherapy and participated in every form of self-improvement I came upon, but nothing ever made it go away for good. It was senseless. And what I discovered when I went to graduate school in psychology was that there still was no good explanation for the type of depression I suffered from. It seemed like it had always been a part of me, a dark, painful force I couldn't control.

I can recall being depressed even as a very young child. Picture a cute little waif of an eight-year-old girl dutifully brushing her teeth before bedtime. She crawls into her bed with her stuffed toys, and receives a kiss goodnight from her mother who turns out the lights. The little girl lies awake in bed, staring at the ceiling and prays, "Please don't let me wake up in the morning." Why would a little child have such dark thoughts? Night after night I did. And every morning I was bummed to wake up and find out I was still alive, and to add insult to injury, I had to go to school.

My childhood depression worsened as I grew into an adolescent and changed in quality as I became an adult, but it was always there. When I would look back on the history of my depression to try to make sense of it, there was none to be found. There was absolutely no reason I should have ever become so depressed in the first place. I wasn't abused. We weren't living in poverty. I didn't have any learning disabilities or physical ailments. It was a mystery without a solution until I began thinking about it in a radically different way.

Empathic ability provided an entirely new way of thinking about emotions. My lifetime depression didn't make any sense, just like the depression I experienced from Dan and the apathy from Gary. That had to be it. My entire life I had been empathic, but didn't realize it. I had been feeling other people's emotional pain from the beginning. I cannot fully convey to you the relief I felt when I first had this thought. It was like the weight of a thousand lifetimes had been lifted from my shoulders. The thought rang true like a crystal bell. This was the explanation for a lifetime of senseless emotional agony and suffering.

I don't think that my recurrent depression was directly caused by an empathic link to someone every single time I felt depressed. But I do believe that empathy was the foundation of the continued depressive episodes. Here is the process that I feel sure took place. Put simply, during childhood I became so used to feeling painful emotions, that I developed my own depression. I think that around that age when you start intellectually identifying yourself and your personality, around age 7, that I was well aware I was often sad and depressed. We learn at a young age that the emotions we feel come from within ourselves. Where else would they be coming from? Therefore, throughout my childhood as I developed, I identified any empathic feelings as coming from my own mind, taking ownership of the emotions and developing my own depression in response. That never ending cycle fueled the chronic depression I suffered from for over 25 years.

I had had the greatest revelation of my life. The mystery of my emotional struggles was over. I also had found the key flower essence to help me manage my empathic ability, which was called Yarrow. I felt stronger than I had in years. I understood how empathy had impacted the circumstances of my life. The only reason I suffered so much emotional torment over the years was because I didn't know anything about the existence of empathic ability. I realized that there had to be many, many people out there just like me who were suffering because our society doesn't teach us about psychic or inexplicable phenomena. Without any knowledge of empathy, how could we control it?

When I worked as a psychologist, I saw numerous people with symptoms like mine. Unrelenting depression or anxiety haunted them their entire lives. These patients never were entirely helped by psychotherapy or medication. Now I realized that it was likely that they were empathic too. Through all my struggles and research, I never did explain my empathic experiences to anyone. The time to start talking has come.

Chapter 2

Depression & Emotional Sensitivity

Depression

For those of you who suffer from depression, or know someone who does, I don't need to define what it is for you. You are intimately familiar with the pain, the dark bleakness, the hopelessness, the tears, the self-defeating thoughts that won't go away, and the suicidal desires that seem like the only escape. Depression is a serious and very real affliction. One only has to look at the multi million-dollar sales of Prozac and other anti-depressants to grasp the magnitude of this problem.

There are several causes of depression. Most stem back to childhood, such as abuse, growing up with an alcoholic parent, or not receiving adequate love and care. There are all sorts of childhood and family dysfunctions that can leave a person feeling empty into adulthood. Other causes related to depression are grief and loss, trauma, marital and relationship problems, and societal pressures. Psychologists have a good understanding of the type of experiences that can lead to depression. We also understand how depression can develop into a chronic psychological disorder over the course of a person's lifetime. With all this understanding, you would think that we would be able to help any depressed person who walked in the door. But this is not the case. Countless people suffer from chronic depression that defies traditional treatments. There is a possible cause that we have missed.

In my story in Chapter One I shared with you how I suffered from horrible, recurrent depression for years. I tried everything to get rid of it. I went through psychotherapy. I addressed issues from childhood. I worked through adult relationship problems that were causing me serious difficulty. At the time it seemed like I must be getting to the core of my depression. Once I worked through all these issues, there would be no more reason to be depressed. Or so I thought.

One of the most memorable and saddest depressive episodes I can recall happened a few months after I got married. I had worked through every conceivable childhood conflict in therapy. I had long since solved my troublesome relationship patterns. My self-esteem was better than it had ever been. I had met and married the sweet, wonderful man of my dreams. And there I lay in the middle of the floor, tears streaming from my eyes, wishing I could die.

I was furious. How could this possibly be happening again? There was no logical reason. All the issues I worked through had contributed to my recurrent depression, but apparently they weren't really the underlying cause. I was overcome. There was no place else to look for answers, nowhere to turn. I was defeated. It seemed I was doomed to suffer from depression no matter what I did. All I could do was wait for this depressive episode to pass, and hope the next one didn't come too soon. I had exhausted all the resources I knew of at the time.

Several years later I when I had my empathic experiences, it turned my world upside down. I was horrified to be feeling other people's emotional pain. Hadn't I been through enough? Didn't I have enough of my own pain without experiencing other people's as well? It took me a while to realize that what had seemed to turn my life upside-down was actually turning it right side up. I was being shown in a very blatant manner what I needed to see. These empathic experiences weren't anything new. They weren't adding extra pain on top of my own suffering as I had originally thought. They were a profound demonstration of empathy in action, so I could finally become aware of the reason for my lifelong depression. The depression and suffering I called my own rarely had been. I had been feeling the pain and intensity of the world around me, not from within my own psyche. The world didn't make me depressed. I felt the depression of the world. Empathy was a radically different idea about the source of painful emotions and psychological disorders.

Once I was aware of empathy, I thought about all the clients and other people I knew who suffered from depression. I wondered how many of them were empathic? Due to life circumstances, how many of them had developed layers of their own depression on top of their empathic ability? How many of them knew a phenomenon like psychic feeling was even possible, much less a part of them? On the other hand, how many of them were not empathic, but were solely depressed in direct response to their own life issues? To casually observe a person's depressive symptoms, it would be nearly impossible to tell. I reasoned that there had to be other psychological indicators of empathic ability in addition to diffuse or recurrent depression.

What were the traits that would always point to empathic ability? If I could figure this out, empathy would become a more tangible and easily identifiable concept. People would be able to know with certainty that they were empathic. I knew not every empathic person would have extreme experiences like I did to make their empathy obvious to them. The majority would be like I had been for most of the years of my life, completely unaware of empathy. If I could identify the psychological and behavioral traits of empathic ability, it would serve several purposes. People would have more solid footing to begin understanding the effects of empathy on their lives. Empathic people would have tangible evidence of their psychic feeling abilities. If empathy could be connected with more conventional behavior, it wouldn't seem like such a strange or scary subject. People would feel more comfortable talking about it. Finding the common psychological denominator of empathy became the next step in my research.

I began collecting case studies of people who had had empathic experiences, and found that the answer I was seeking was not far from view. Empathic people do have observable traits that are easily identified. Interestingly, the traits are a set of characteristics that have always had their own air of mystery. I'm referring to a set of psychological traits that has never been adequately explained before. These characteristics are commonly referred to as emotional sensitivity.

Emotional Sensitivity

Sensitivity is a set of character traits that has just begun receiving attention from the psychological community within the past few years. This is strange because it has always been fairly prevalent among the population. Nevertheless, it has not even been officially recognized as a personality type. I want to make sure that you understand what I mean when I use the term sensitivity. Following is a list that describes the attributes of emotionally sensitive people.

1. Emotionally sensitive people feel emotions often and deeply. They feel as if they "wear their emotions on their sleeves."

2. They are keenly aware of the emotions of people around them.

3. Sensitive people are easily hurt or upset. An insult or unkind remark will affect them deeply.

4. In a similar vein, sensitive people strive to avoid conflicts. They dread arguments and other types of confrontations because the negativity affects them so much.

5. Sensitive people are not able to shake off emotions easily. Once they are saddened or upset by something, they cannot just switch gears and forget it.

6. Sensitive people are greatly affected by emotions they witness. They feel deeply for others' suffering. Many sensitive people avoid sad movies or watching the news because they cannot bear the weighty emotions that would drive to their core and stick with them afterwards.

7. Sensitive people are prone to suffer from recurrent depression, anxiety or other psychological disorders.

8. On the positive side, sensitive people are also keenly aware of and affected by beauty in art, music and nature. They are the world's greatest artists and art appreciators.

9. Sensitive people are prone to stimulus overload. That is, they can't stand large crowds, loud noise, or hectic environments. They feel overwhelmed and depleted by too much stimuli.

10. Sensitive people are born that way. They were sensitive children. There are a couple different responses kids have to their sensitivity. One type of sensitive child is the stereotypical kid who gets picked on by bullies, and is a well-behaved, good student because she cannot stand the thought of getting into trouble. The other type of sensitive child more often experiences the stimulus overload mentioned in the previous paragraph. These children are thus over stimulated and have difficulty focusing, which causes them problems in school.

Sensitive people typically exhibit all or nearly all of the above descriptors.

One of the sure signs of a truly sensitive person is that he feels animosity toward his sensitive nature. Most sensitive people whole-heartedly wish they were tougher and more thick-skinned. They feel like their sensitivity is a weakness. They wish things didn't bother them so much. They wish their emotions weren't so obvious to other people. They wish they could let things go and not worry so much. They aren't comfortable with their sensitivity, and wish they could do something to get rid of it (or at least get rid of the negative aspects of it). Therefore, some sensitive adults have learned how to hide their sensitivity from others.

Sensitivity occurs just as often in males as it does in females. But our culture teaches men that they are to be tough, not sensitive. So men are the ones who learn more quickly how to mask their sensitivity. They hide it and repress it, but they still cannot make it go away. They remain deeply affected by emotions. These men who mask their sensitivity are actually affected even more deeply by their sensitivity because they internalize feelings, rather than expressing them. This increases their suffering from more generalized emotional pain in the form of depression or anxiety. These men are well aware that they are sensitive. They would admit it in a therapeutic relationship or when reading this book, but they are so practiced in hiding it that many of their friends and coworkers would not know it. Women, on the other hand, are freer to express emotions, and thus do not have such pressure to hide their sensitivity. Some women still do, though, because of career roles or simply because they are tired of feeling sensitive all the time.

Now we should be on the same wavelength about exactly what I am referring to when I use the term sensitivity. In some respects it is a vague concept, but people who are sensitive will have no problem identifying themselves in the above discussion. Sensitivity has always been relegated to the outskirts of psychology. The traits of sensitivity are not considered to be symptoms of a psychological disorder, nor should they be. Yet they also have never been identified in their entirety as representative of a personality type. That is to say, in tradi-tional psychological literature there is no such thing as the sensitive personality. In modern thought, sensitivity hovers somewhere between the two. Sensitivity seems to consist of character traits that make a person more susceptible to emotional difficulties. This is how it appears from a conventional viewpoint.

On the whole, psychologists don't know what to do with a sensitive patient. Sensitive people often go to therapy to try to understand themselves. They think something must be wrong with them because they are so affected by emotions. But, sadly, their sensitivity is usually overlooked by the psychologist who does not have a frame of reference for it. Emphasis is put on other issues such as the sensitive patient's depression, anxiety, job stress or marital difficulties. The therapist may turn the focus to assertiveness training or reducing self-defeating thoughts. These are all important issues, but when they are addressed outside of the context of the person's sensitivity, it doesn't do the patient much good in the long term.

A case example will demonstrate what I mean.

Janelle

Janelle was a young, attractive black woman. She was an extremely sensitive person who was agitated and anxious most of the time. She had a physical disability and one leg was shorter than the other. This caused her to limp, which she was very embarrassed about. (It was hardly noticeable to the casual observer.) She was stressed about her job as a marketing assistant. She was overwhelmed that she was not getting along with her new roommate. She was nearly having panic attacks about mice in her house. To top it all off, she had recently been mugged, and that was causing her all sorts of anger, worry and stress.

Janelle's counselor did not know where to begin with her. To simplify things, he tried focusing on one issue at a time. They began with the mugging because that was an acute event that had just happened. The counselor tried to help Janelle rationally analyze the mugging and identify things she could do to protect herself in the future. In the next sessions, they focused on Janelle's problems with her roommate because that was a pervasive issue that was causing her a lot of grief. They talked about that for a few sessions, identifying Janelle's role in the relationship, her own responsibilities as a roommate, and what she could and couldn't control about it. They seemed to be making some progress at first, but soon their discussions were going around in circles. Janelle's phobic fear of mice in her house increased. Janelle came for a couple more therapy sessions, but soon stopped coming because she was not feeling any different. She didn't feel understood. Janelle's counselor was just as frustrated. He was overwhelmed by all her symptoms. He felt like he didn't help her much, but he didn't know what he could have done any differently.

This is an extreme example because Janelle was such an intensely sensitive person. But because of that it clearly shows how Janelle's situation did not change because the underlying foundation of her struggles, emotional sensitivity, was neither identified nor addressed. Her counselor was never taught to recognize sensitivity, nor was he trained in any therapeutic methods that address it. Most counselors and therapists are equally uninformed about sensitivity. Why is it that such a common set of traits is so mysterious to the people who make it their business to understand emotions and behavior?

It is because sensitivity is beyond the black and white boundaries of psychological disorder vs. "normal" behavior. Sensitivity lies in a realm that cannot be explained by conventional psychological theories. It can't be directly correlated to past trauma, abuse or family dysfunction. Some recent theories have been put forth that sensitivity is due to an overactive nervous system, or to put it another way, that sensitive people's nervous systems are in a state of hyper-arousal. This statement is not an explanation of the underlying cause of sensitivity. The gaping question it leaves unanswered is "Why is the sensitive person's nervous system in a constant state of arousal?" The answer to this question won't be found in traditional medical or psychological theories. But I did find the answer in my research of empathic ability.

While gathering case studies, I quickly realized that emotional sensitivity was the common factor. Empathy, or psychic feeling, is the underlying cause of sensitivity. Alternately, to make this point absolutely clear, if a person has the traits of emotional sensitivity that indicates, without a doubt, that she has empathic ability. Sensitive people empathically experience the emotions of those around them.

Sensitivity starts to make much more sense from this vantage point. Sensitive people feel intense emotions, are aware of others' feelings, are deeply impacted by others' emotions, and can't shake off painful feelings because all these things are directly due to empathy.

Since our society does not teach us about empathic ability or even acknowledge that it exists, sensitive people have no way to understand or process the emotions they empathically sense from others. They have no means to control or manage their empathic ability. The painful, empathic emotions build up over time, and manifest as some of the less desirable traits of sensitivity, which are being easily hurt, not being able to shake off emotions, fear of conflict, suffering from depression or anxiety, and lastly, feeling stimulus overload in crowded or loud places. This last experience appears to directly relate to the hyper-aroused nervous system. Sensitive people's nervous systems are aroused because their empathic ability is out of whack. They are being bombarded by too many empathic feelings too often. The nervous system does what it can to register and process all the emotional input, but it can't keep up. Hence, sensitive people's nervous systems are stressed and agitated by too much to do.

Since sensitive, empathic people are constantly feeling other people's emotions, it's no wonder that they feel overloaded with emotions. They are experiencing more emotions than any one person should. These folks can intimately sense within themselves the emotional energies in the environment around them. This is why they become overwhelmed in crowded, busy places. While interviewing empathic people, I found it interesting that many of them used the same words to describe their experiences. They said they felt like "an emotional sponge." They used this term to explain that they felt like they soaked up emotions from the crowd around them. The problem was when they got home, they didn't know how to wring themselves out.

I want to make it clear that there are a few traits of sensitivity that do not relate to being negatively overwhelmed by empathy. Sensitive people are emotional creatures. They are aware of their own emotions. They are also empathic in the most basic sense of the word, being keenly aware of other's emotions. People feel understood around an empathic person. Many sensitive people gravitate toward the helping and healing professions because they naturally understand other's emotions. Lastly, sensitive people are great appreciators of art and often have artistic ability. Their empathic ability allows them to sense the depth and meaning of art. These traits of sensitivity are all highly desirable. What a cold, nasty world it would be without people to understand emotions, connect with other's emotions, and create and appreciate art.

These three desirable traits are the only true traits of sensitivity and empathic ability. Hold on, and I'll explain what I mean by that. The other less desirable traits of sensitivity that we discussed above (easily hurt and overwhelmed, a prevalence of negative emotions, depression and anxiety, and stimulus overload) are all signs of empathy gone wrong. They manifest only when empathy has been ignored and unmanaged. The build up of painful empathic emotions over time causes these negative traits of sensitivity. They are not the natural, intended characteristics of sensitivity. This leads to an important point.

Once the sensitive person gains knowledge about empathy and learns how to release and heal his empathically sensed emotions, he no longer will experience the undesirable traits of sensitivity. All that will be left are the three desirable ones. This is a radical idea. Although people don't understand sensitivity, they assume that it is not changeable. Common thought dictates that a sensitive person is forever sensitive, doomed to be hurt, overwhelmed and overloaded her entire life. This is absolutely not true. With information about the existence of empathy and healing of the years of empathic build up, a sensitive person will be rid of the negative traits of sensitivity, just like she has always wished she could be.

In summary, the positive traits of sensitivity are purely indicators of empathic ability. The undesirable characteristics of sensitivity, including recurrent depression, are caused by empathy gone awry due to lack of information and guidance. In our present day society, since so few people have any knowledge of empathy, most sensitive people suffer from the bad along with the good. They are not even aware of their empathic ability, much less have any idea how to control it. While researching empathy, I found that emotional sensitivity was the psychological, observable manifestation of psychic feeling ability. When you get right down to it, the words *empathy and sensitivity* refer to the same thing. A sensitive person is empathic, and an empathic person is sensitive.

I looked up the word sensitive in my Webster's dictionary and found the following definitions: 1. able to respond to a very slight stimulus, keenly aware of the moods and feelings of others, easily hurt, readily affected by the feelings of others, quick to react to external influences. Then I read the second definition of sensitive: 2. a person with psychic abilities. Who knew it had been in the dictionary on the bookshelf all along?

Emotional Sensitivity in Children

Wouldn't it have been great when you were a sensitive child if someone would have taken you aside, explained to you that you were empathic, and taught you all about it? You would have learned how to control your empathy and how to protect yourself from taking on too many painful emotions. Well, it's not too late to do those things for yourself now as an adult, but just think about how much smoother your life would have been if you had learned about empathy when you were younger. For those of you who have a sensitive child, you can do this for her. All the concepts in this book apply just as well to children as they do to adults.

I was a very sensitive little girl. I was the stereotypical kid I described earlier who was picked on by everybody. I was easily moved to tears by a sad song or movie. I could hardly enjoy some of the standard childhood entertainment. "Bambi's mother just died! I can't watch this anymore." I spent a lot of time playing alone in my room. My childhood depression that I spoke of in chapter one was not obvious to my parents. I kept it to myself. I was a quiet, good student. I seemed perfectly all right to the casual observer, but I was in a lot of pain. I was overwhelmed by negative emotions most of the time.

As I alluded to in the previous section about sensitivity, not all children respond to their empathic ability in the same way I did. Some children feel more of the hyper-aroused nervous system and stimulus overload. They have difficulty focusing and may seem scattered. I believe that my nervous system was also hyper-aroused, but my reaction was to be exhausted by it. I was always tired. I hardly ever felt upbeat excitement for anything, even when I was happy, because my nervous system was depleted. Other children may respond differently. They will feel more agitated or revved by the constant state of hyper-arousal. This will lead them to behave impulsively, be overexciteable, moody, and find it very difficult to focus on one thing at a time. They may be anxious, edgy children, or they may be hyperactive and labeled with attention deficit disorder.

In regard to attention deficit, the common approach to treatment is for the diagnosed child to take Ritalin. Ritalin is a stimulant. The prevalent theory as to why Ritalin seemingly calms hyperactive children is that it further stimulates the already hyper nervous system, causing it to overload and shut down in some respects. So it makes sense why it appears to help the sensitive, empathic child. The Ritalin creates additional stimulus to the nervous system, interfering with the child's ability to sense psychic feelings. From this perspective, Ritalin is a short term band-aid. It does not address empathy, which is the true underlying cause of the child's sensitivity, and unfairly chemically inhibits the child's empathic ability. Attention deficit is a complex topic, but I wanted to mention it because it is very relevant to sensitivity and empathy. This topic deserves more coverage than I can fully give it in this book, which is about sensitivity and empathy in general. Visit my website at www.KyraMesich.com for other books that focus on childhood issues and attention deficit disorder more specifically.

So, as a parent, how do you know if your child's symptoms are due to empathic ability? Children cannot verbally convey their emotional experiences very clearly. It's not likely that your child will be able to say, "My friend Sammy's dog died, and it made me feel so sad it was as if my own dog had died. And I couldn't stop feeling sad about it, even when we started playing a game." It's much more likely that your child will seem sad. You'll ask him what's wrong, and he'll shrug his shoulders with the standard reply, "I don't know." Luckily, you can look to more observable behaviors and for an indication. If your child is the stereotypical sensitive type of kid (emotional, easily hurt, picked on at school, and often seems upset or depressed), then that is all the evidence you need. Your child is sensitive and has empathic ability.

Donnie

Donnie was a 12-year-old boy who was a quiet, sensitive kid and a good student. He had blue eyes and brown, scruffy hair that managed to look unkempt no matter how much it was brushed. His posture was a perpetual slouch, and his eyes were cast downward most of the time. Donnie was recently diagnosed as nearsighted, so he had new eyeglasses that he was very self-conscious about wearing. He loved playing with his computer and reading. These two hobbies took up most of his afternoons and evenings. His parents tried to get him involved in sports and other group activities so he could make friends and learn to be more outgoing. Most of the time Donnie really wasn't interested. He often said he didn't feel like going to practice and wanted to stay home. Donnie was moody a lot of the time, but could never explain what he was upset about. His mother was frustrated about what to do for him.

Donnie had a close, positive relationship with his father. Unfortunately, his dad suffered from depression and experienced depressive episodes several times a year. Donnie worried a lot about his dad's depression. He couldn't stand to see his father seem so sad.

Let's dissect Donnie's case and take a closer look at what is going on for him. He exhibits characteristics of emotional sensitivity. He feels emotions deeply, worries for others' well being, and is moody and withdrawn. These traits of sensitivity indicate that Donnie is empathic. Since he is empathic, that means he has experiences of feeling other people's emotions. This is a good part of the reason that he shies away from group activities. After being in school all day, he has already been exposed to a lot of emotional energy. He is the type of sensitive child who needs to rest for a little while after being in a group. He is not ready to go straight from school into another group activity. It would emotionally wear him out.

Donnie is moody. He is often upset, irritable or sad, but does not know why. His moodiness is not always a reaction to events in school. Sometimes it just seems to hit him out of the blue. This is a sign that Donnie has been taking on a lot of emotional energies from others. He is feeling other people's emotional pain, but then has no way to understand it or relieve it. This is confusing to him and further adds to the moodiness. When a child is frequently depressed, anxious or irritable for no apparent reason, he is feeling those emotions from someone, and generally it is from close family and friends.

In Donnie's case, it is clear that he is greatly affected by his father's depression. But Donnie feels much more than sympathy for his father's suffering. He literally feels his father's emotional pain within himself. This is a typical scenario. Sensitive children have their first empathic experiences with the people who are closest to them, their family. From this statement, it might seem like I am saying that poor sensitive Donnie is doomed to feel his father's emotional pain for his entire life. That is not true.

Luckily, there is much that Donnie can be taught about his empathic ability. Simple methods and healing remedies can make him much more aware of his empathy, and teach him the how to manage it, so he will not be vulnerable to feeling other's pain. He can learn to protect himself from stimulus overload. Then he would not feel so drained by groups and would have more fun participating in after school activities. We will revisit Donnie in Chapter 4 where I'll explain exactly what healing remedies and approaches achieved these goals.

Donnie is the stereotypical type of sensitive, empathic child who grows up to be an emotionally sensitive adult. As I mentioned above, some children respond differently to the empathic emotions they are experiencing. They may seem more obviously depressed, anxious or over-aroused. The remaining chapters in this book will explain more about empathy and how it manifests, which should help you be able to identify whether your child's symptoms are related to empathic ability.

In this chapter I explained how chronic psychological distress, emotional sensitivity and empathic ability are all related. Empathic ability is at the root of psychological distress much more often than you might think. This is a radically new way of conceptualizing our emotional experiences. Empathic ability finally explains some of the most confusing and previously incurable psychological struggles. This new idea has probably left you with a lot of questions about empathy. What exactly is empathic ability? How does it work? Your questions will be answered in the next chapter, which discusses empathy in more detail and gives examples of some of the different types of empathic experiences.

Chapter 3

Empathy

Empathy is the purest form of emotional communication. It is the language of emotion. It is a necessary form of communication in order for humans to live together in harmony. We need to be able to clearly convey emotion, to empathize with each other's emotional experiences, and understand the emotional reasons behind people's behaviors. Empathy is the means by which we were intended to be able to easily do these things. Without empathy, we are left with only our intellect to try to make sense of emotions. This is why we presently have such difficulty explaining our feelings or understanding others' emotional responses. The intellect was not meant to be the primary way we communicate about emotions. Empathy exists for this purpose.

Empathy developed early on in human evolution. It would have been necessary to develop empathy when human lifestyle changed from solitary survival of the fittest to survival within and for the group. Family and tribe developed, and we became social creatures. In the present day, from family to work, church, neighborhood, town, and country, we remain connected to and inter-dependent on groups for our survival. It makes sense that humans evolved to be able to create harmony and understanding within their complex groups. Empathy maintains the emotional connection among people who need to work together in a group, whether it is a small family, tribe, or large governing body. The problem is that empathy is an ability that has gone by the wayside while humans have focused on the development of intellect, industry and science in our recent history.

Intellectual communication dominates in our present day society. This is the language of ideas, science and industry. We are all masters of intellectual communication. From years of schooling and practice, we can easily and precisely convey ideas and concepts with words or mathematics. A focus on intellectual communication was necessary for us to reach the physical achievements that have been accomplished in recent history. Understanding the laws of physics, chemistry, creating huge power grids, telecommunications technology, building cars and a complex network of roads, skyscrapers, air travel, money, computers and the internet—none of these things would exist without mastery of intellectual communication. We have developed intellectual communication to its greatest extent. We focused on intellect so completely that we have forgotten we also have another form of communication available to us.

There are two basic modes of communication in which humans could be fluent. They are the language of intellect and the language of emotion. They are separate because they function differently. Intellect is a projective language. We use it to send out ideas. Intellectual communication occurs only when a person intends to send a message. Years of learning are required during our childhoods in order to master the sophisticated intellectual language we use today.

Emotional language is based in empathy. Empathy is a receptive language that is sensed internally. We receive others' emotional communication, whether they intend to send it or not. We are born with a natural ability for empathic communication. Emotional communication is not superior to our prevalent intellectual language and vice versa. These two methods of communication are different and serve different purposes. They are both needed in human society.

Unfortunately, in our present day society we only learn about intellectual communication. We grow up learning our intellectual language and are never taught that empathic, emotional communication even exists. We are forced to translate our emotional experiences into intellectual language, resulting in miscommunication and misunderstandings. We all are born with empathic ability. This natural form of emotional communication still exists within us, even though we don't learn about it. Because empathic communication is ignored, disregarded and repressed in our culture, one of two things can happen. The empathic ability weakens over time or it becomes distorted.

For the sake of this discussion let's say that 50% of children are born with an average empathic ability and 50% are born with a strong empathic ability. For the children who are born with an average ability, their empathy weakens over the years as the focus is placed solely on their intellectual development. The children who are born with strong empathic ability have a different experience. From the time they are babies they can easily sense other people's emotions, and continue to do so throughout their childhood. But without any guidance or information about empathy, they have no way to categorize or understand the empathic emotions they feel. This leads to a kid and eventually an adult who experiences a lot of emotions and is confused as to why and where they are coming from. Their empathy does not weaken over time because they are continually using it. There are tons of emotions all around them to empathically sense all the time. They don't know how to turn off, control or manage empathy, so it just continues working without any rest.

It's akin to how music becomes distorted when you turn it up too loud. Turn up the volume on your stereo as loud as it will go, and your speakers will emit a lot of distortion. Fine notes and nuances are lost. Clarity is overtaken by fuzziness. All that is left is a primitive sketch of the intent of the song. This is the same experience that occurs for highly empathic people. Their empathy is constantly wide open to receive input. Over time they continue to receive more and more emotional input from the people around them. With no way to release or process the emotions they receive, and more and more coming in all the time, they eventually reach full volume. Their empathy becomes distorted just like the speakers from too much input. What they sense after that is the most intense, primitive and loudest emotions.

This point answers the most common question I receive about empathy, which is "Why do empathic people only sense painful, negative emotions from others?" Some sensitive people wonder if something is wrong with them because they only seem to pick up on emotional pain and suffering. If empathy is simply the ability to feel others' emotions, then shouldn't an empathic person be equally affected by positive as well as negative feelings? This is a true statement when empathy is healthy and balanced, but consider what I've just said in the previous paragraph.

Psychic feeling becomes distorted for strongly empathic people because it is always fully open and ready to receive. Too much information bombards the highly empathic person because she is never taught how to refine and develop her empathic abilities. More and more emotional input comes in until full volume and distortion is reached. At that point, the empathic person picks up on the loudest, most intense, primitive emotions. These are the most painful emotions humans experience, anger, despair, and fear. It is possible that the distorted empathy could pick up on an intense positive emotion, such as extreme excitement. But, the sad fact is that it is much, much rarer to see an intensely happy person, than it is to come into contact with a very tense, depressed or anxious person. That's just the odds in our unhappy world, which makes it that much harder on the empathic person.

Empathy is not intended to be painful or to be confused with our own emotions. It is intended to be nothing more than a form of emotional communication that we all could use in a safe and protected manner. Unfortunately, we have lost awareness of our ability for emotional communication due to a sole focus on the development of the intellect. That leaves empathy to either deteriorate or become distorted.

When empathy weakens, it leads to people who depend totally on their intellect for their survival. They are disconnected from their own emotions and do not understand other people's emotional reactions. Emotions seem like a strange, completely illogical landscape that can never be safely traversed. When empathy becomes distorted, it causes people to be overwhelmed by emotion. Being overwhelmed by emotion in an intellectual world is seen as an embarrassment and a liability, which causes sensitive people to identify themselves as weak when they are not. They have perplexing empathic experiences, which can't be explained from an intellectual standpoint. These empathic experiences can take several different forms.

Sandra

Sandra was a secretary who accepted a new job working in the offices of a large hospital. Shortly after accepting her new position, she began feeling depressed and tense most of the time. She reasoned that it must be due to the stress of starting a new job. Then one day, Sandra became fully aware of the source of her tension. As she walked the long corridors through the hospital back to her car, she was hit by the solemnness and tension that hung thick in the air. As she passed by sick patients, rushed nurses, and worried visitors, her stomach tightened. She could literally feel the angst emanating from nearly every person there. By the time she finally reached her car, she was emotionally exhausted. She burst into tears. Sandra was overwhelmed by the painful emotions she felt from so many people in the hospital. She started her car, and wondered how she would be able to continue working there.

John

John was a 50-year-old mid-level manager in an airline corporation. The airline was anticipating a merger, so his workdays were insanely busy. On one particular day he had felt a nagging pit of depression all afternoon, but didn't have time to give in to it. He was on the phone or in meetings constantly. When his day finally started to slow down, he realized he was starving. He needed to order some Chinese food for delivery. He figured he would dictate a couple memos, eat some dinner, and then have a relaxing drive home. He called Chin's, and ordered his usual with an extra egg roll. After he hung up the phone, he noticed that everything was quiet. Most everyone else had left for the day. The silence was unusual but very pleasant. Then John was suddenly overtaken by the depression he had been pushing aside all day. He felt the urge to cry. "What the hell is wrong with me," he thought to himself, "Am I that stressed?"

He shook his head, and picked up the phone to call his wife to let her know when he would be home. She didn't answer, so he decided to check the answering machine messages. There was a message from his wife reminding him that this was the night for her pottery class, so he would have to get his own dinner. The next message was from the tailor, saying that his pants were ready to be picked up. Then there was a message from Helen, one of John's best friends for years. Helen's voice cracked as she said that she really needed to talk with John. She had just found out that afternoon that her son had died in an accident. John hung up the phone. He was stunned. He called Helen back right then and talked with her about her son's accident. After their conversation John leaned back and pondered, was it Helen's grief that he had felt? He sympathized with Helen's loss, but he could tell that the depression and urge to cry he had previously felt were now gone.

Gabbie

Gabbie was a 10 year old, energetic, talkative little girl. Her parents were sociable people who frequently had parties and gatherings in their home. Usually the same friends and acquaintances came to their gatherings, but on one night a new person named Greg came as a guest of a guest. As a rule, Gabbie liked to participate in her parents' parties and would become the center of attention more than once during the evening. But on this night she was reserved and stayed near the family's closest friends and her dog, Rusty.

After everyone left, Mom said to Gabbie, "You sure were quiet tonight. Are you feeling all right?" Gabbie quickly replied, "Will that guy be coming back to our house again?" "What guy?" Mom asked, a bit startled. "That new guy. Will he be coming to any more of our parties?" Dad interjected, "She must mean Greg." "Oh," replied Mom, "Well, I don't know, Hon. He knows some of our friends, so he might. He seemed nice enough. Why do you ask?" "I don't like him," Gabbie said bluntly. "Why not?" asked Mom. "I don't know. I just don't like him. Rusty didn't like him either," Gabbie said softly. "Well, you have to have a better reason than that," chided Dad. Mom took Gabbie aside and told her, "Next time I'll ask people to let me know if they're bringing a guest, so we'll know who's coming. Okay?" "Okay," said Gabbie feeling a little more comfortable.

A few weeks later Gabbie's parents found out that Greg had been arrested for cocaine trafficking. He had a history of other criminal activity, including some violent crimes. None of his current friends had any idea about this other side of his life. It seemed like he had fooled everyone. Gabbie's parents thought about asking Gabbie how she knew, but then they thought better of it.

All of these stories are examples of empathy in action, but you'll notice they had different qualities. Sandra could feel the painful emotions of all the people around her. John felt his friend's grief even though he was not in physical proximity of her. Gabbie did not feel emotions, per se. But while the adults based their opinion of Greg on his outward behavior, Gabbie felt the true quality of his character.

All three of these examples demonstrate how empathy is emotional communication. Sandra became overwhelmed because she felt inundated from too much emotional information from all the people around her. If John had been more aware of his empathic ability, he would have realized sooner that he needed to contact his friend Helen. Gabbie's story shows how empathy can provide very useful information. She sensed that Greg was trouble. How did she know? Greg communicated it to her in a way that couldn't be heard intellectually, but could easily be sensed empathically.

In the remaining chapters of this book we'll discuss how to ease empathy so that it does not feel so painfully overwhelming as in Sandra's case. You'll learn how to be more aware of empathic communication, which will prevent you from confusing it with your own emotions like John did. Lastly, we'll discuss how to positively develop empathy for the useful information it can provide, such as was demonstrated by Gabbie.

That's a lot of ground we have yet to cover, but we'll take it one step at a time. We'll begin by discussing how the painful aspects of sensitivity can be alleviated. Many people experience the essence of their sensitivity as a feeling of vulnerability. They don't feel protected from the negativity and intensity of the world around them. This is the core issue of sensitivity. How can you interact with people and your environment without being hurt or overwhelmed?

I have found the answer to this question with an alternative health remedy called flower essences. The next chapter contains detailed information about flower essences since these remedies address the core issue of sensitivity. In Chapter 4 you'll learn what flower essences are, how they are used, and how they can heal the hurt and emotional overwhelm that sensitive, empathic people so often feel.

Chapter 4

Flower Essences

This chapter is going to teach you all about flower essences, a very healing remedy for sensitive people. There is a lot of information we will cover including what flower essences are, how they are used, and which ones work the best to rebalance your empathic ability so that it no longer causes depression or the painful symptoms of emotional sensitivity.

When I first realized that empathic ability was the basis of my confusing emotional experiences, lifelong depression, and emotional sensitivity, that was just the beginning of my search. Understanding that empathy was the underlying cause of my difficulties was not sufficient to control it or heal the effects of years of emotional confusion. Knowledge in and of itself was the starting point, not the end. It takes more than an intellectual understanding of empathy to heal and release years of empathic emotion. Having the knowledge that empathy exists does not automatically enlighten you as to how to control it in the future. Most of us have a lifetime of complete ignorance about the existence of empathic ability to overcome. I continued searching for the most effective remedies and techniques that would help empathic people. The results of that search are contained in this chapter and Chapter 5.

Chapter 5 will discuss meditation as a means for connecting with your empathic ability, but I have repeatedly found in my work with sensitive people that the best approach is to start with flower essences. They are the remedy that has had the most overall profoundly beneficial impact for sensitive people. Flower essences can rebalance your empathic ability, release years of painful empathic emotion, and help you feel more protected and less overwhelmed by your sensitivity. Without any further ado, let's begin by discussing what flower essences are.

Flower essences

Flower essences are an alternative health remedy that is used specifically for emotional healing. They have gained a great deal of popularity over the past few years and can be purchased in most any health food store or herb shop. Flower essences, also called flower remedies, are made from the blooms of specific flowering plants and trees. Please note that flower essences are completely different from essential oils used in aromatherapy. Flower essences are similar to homeopathic remedies and are in liquid form. They have hardly any smell or taste, and the dosage is a very small amount taken several times per day. The flower essence liquid is traditionally preserved with a small amount of brandy, but essences preserved with vinegar or glycerin are available for those who are not tolerant of alcohol. Flower essences do not have medicinal side effects. They will not interfere with other medications or remedies you may be taking. Since they are gentle and side effect free, essences are an ideal remedy for children. Essences are taken orally by putting a couple drops in a small glass of water.

Flower essences facilitate significant beneficial changes emotionally and mentally, which also lead to physical benefits. Flower essences are so useful for emotional sensitivity that it is almost as though they were made exactly for the issue of empathic ability. Amazingly, there are many flower essences that specifically address the needs of sensitive people. Flower essences are like herbal remedies in that there are hundreds to choose from. To keep things simple, we are going to start with the three most important flower remedies I have found. Then you will learn how to choose among all the other flower essences available.

One of the first brands of flower essences I worked with was FES (Flower Essence Society), which is widely available in the United States. It was this brand that had the particular flower essence that provided profound healing for myself and many other empathic people I have helped. That essence is called Yarrow.

Yarrow

Yarrow (*Achillea millefolium*) is a pretty plant that grows commonly in North America. It has finely dissected lacy leaves and flowers in flat clusters. The flower varieties may be white, yellow or pink. Yarrow has been known for centuries as a strong herbal remedy for cleansing and healing cuts. When Yarrow is made into a flower essence, it has very interesting effects. Yarrow literally rebalances empathy.

Recall from the discussion in the previous chapter that empathy is not intended to be painful or to be confused with our own feelings. Empathy is intended to be emotional communication that we can sense in a protected and safe manner. Yarrow restores that protection and safety to the empathic person. Many empathic people complain that they feel like emotions bombard them no matter what they do. They feel like they have no protection from the negative emotions around them. This is the most vexing problem that sensitive people have as they try to learn and regain control of their empathy. Even though they may understand empathy, they do not know how to stop absorbing other people's painful emotions. Yarrow can change that for the better. Just like herbal Yarrow cleanses and heals the skin after a wound, Yarrow essence heals and rebalances the empathic person's energetic boundaries and natural empathic protection.

After taking Yarrow flower essence, empathic people feel different. They feel less vulnerable and not so bombarded by emotions. They begin to feel more distance from the feelings they do empathically sense, so they no longer confuse empathic emotions with their own feelings. Yarrow essence provides an altogether healing and liberating experience for the empathic person. For many people, it is what really helps them turn the corner to finally be able to control and end the negative effects of their empathic ability.

FES makes Yarrow flower essences from each of the three flower colors. They found that each of the colors has slightly different effects.

White Yarrow (*Simply labeled as Yarrow on the FES bottle.*)

White Yarrow is the most multi-purpose Yarrow essence. It is very beneficial for people who are sensitive to their environment and other people's emotions. It strengthens your energetic boundaries, leaving you more protected from unwanted emotional energy. If you are not sure which essence would be best for you, use White Yarrow.

White Yarrow is the essence I took. Before taking Yarrow flower essence, I was still susceptible to experiencing other people's painful emotions. Even though I understood empathy and was experimenting with other means to learn to control it, such as visualization, I still was not secure. I had reduced the frequency that I felt others' emotions, but it still happened. And it was still an uncomfortable experience for me when it did happen. Yarrow changed the quality of my empathic experiences. I felt safer and more protected. Empathy no longer felt like an invasion. I realized that Yarrow essence was what I had been looking for. It made the process of learning to control my empathic ability incredibly easier from there on out. I took Yarrow essence regularly for a couple months, then occasionally thereafter during stressful times (like when I knew I would be going to a crowded, noisy place or was going to be around a seriously emotionally troubled person). Although I still use flower essences sometimes, I no longer need to take Yarrow. That is how flower essences work. Once it has thoroughly had its beneficial effects for you, its job is done. There is no need to continue taking it.

Pink Yarrow

Pink Yarrow is specifically for those sensitive people who realize they give too much of themselves in relationships. They are compassionate people who are especially vulnerable to absorbing negative emotions from romantic partners, friends and family. Usually in their effort to help friends or family who may be troubled, they wind up taking the painful emotions on themselves.

Alan was a middle-aged male who worked as an adult education instructor. He was a very kind, pleasant person, who seemed to have infinite patience. He was the kind of person who could be referred to as a "caretaker," although some people referred to him in a less flattering way as "a doormat." Alan spent most of his free time doing things for other people. Everyone knew he was the person they could ask for help anytime, no matter how inconvenient it might be for him. He was the friend who would help people move, give them rides while their car was in the shop, and visit them every day with food when they were sick. He also took care of his ailing grandfather. He cared deeply about others and wanted to help people as much as possible. Sometimes it seemed like he cared more about other people than living his own life. He was a very sensitive person, who was frequently overwhelmed with empathic emotion, but he couldn't bring himself to limit contact with some of his most troubled friends and family. He felt like he was the only person who would help them.

Alan is the quintessential compassionate person who benefits from Pink Yarrow. He is so sympathetic to other people's plights that he sacrifices his own needs. In his desire to help others, he is very vulnerable to absorbing their painful emotions. After taking Pink Yarrow for a while, Alan felt more interest in his own life and development. He became aware of some of the relationships that were most destructive for him and was able to greatly reduce or end contact with those people. He remains a very compassionate, caring person, but is not so inclined to take on someone else's suffering as an attempt to help. He became much less overwhelmed by his empathy, and felt, for the first time in his life, that he was actually able to be around people without feeling their pain.

Golden Yarrow

Golden Yarrow is for empathic people who have reacted to their sensitivity by becoming very shy, and avoiding attention or performance situations. They feel imprisoned by their introversion, but do not feel safe enough to increase their social involvement. They have such difficulty coping with their sensitivity that they are inclined to resort to drugs or alcohol in attempt to blunt their senses.

Trish was a 40-year-old, sensitive female who worked in the administrative offices of a huge corporation. She had always been an extremely shy and reserved person. She smoked cigarettes and had a history of alcohol abuse. She tried numerous times to quit both, without much success. She hated her job because there was a lot of deadline pressure, and it was in a giant office complex where thousands of people worked. She felt overwhelmed by the number of people she saw everyday. She suffered from numerous health issues including allergies, back pain, and recurrent digestive problems. She found her emotional sensitivity to be very painful. She felt like there was "something wrong with her" because she was so easily brought to tears and was so affected by other people's comments and moods. She found it easier to avoid contact with people than to deal with the effects of her sensitivity.

Trish's shyness, substance use, and extreme discomfort with her sensitivity indicated that she would be benefited by taking Golden Yarrow. After taking it for a short time, Trish was feeling less affected by other people's moods. This helped her tremendously at work where she had felt that she could not escape other people's emotions. As she continued taking Golden Yarrow, she felt stronger and much more protected. She signed up for an art class she had always wanted to take. She has found it easier to cut back on smoking. Since she no longer feels so overwhelmed and drained by work, she is not so compelled to drink alcohol every evening.

Trish also came to realize that a lot of her physical health problems were related to her struggles with sensitivity. She felt like a lot of her discomfort and fear was internalized, and, thus, developed into physical ailments. All her health difficulties are not cured, but she has been having significantly less problems with back pain and the digestive issues. She continues to make progress, gradually taking more social risks than she has ever felt comfortable doing before. Trish has hope that she will continue making strides in the emotional, social, and physical aspects of her life.

Each person reacts differently to his or her empathic ability. The different Yarrow essences focus in on that. They provide healing for some of the varied responses to sensitivity, with White Yarrow being the most general purpose. All the Yarrow essences are very shielding and protective for those who have to work in hectic, draining environments such as airports, hospitals, and shopping malls.

Other Flower Essences

In addition to Yarrow, there are many, many more kinds of flower essences. There are nearly as many essences as there are flowering plants. That means there are thousands of different essences to choose from overall. It can be daunting to figure out which essence might be most helpful for yourself. That is why I have recommended that you start with Yarrow. It gets to the root of sensitivity by rebalancing empathy and rebuilding your innate protection that was lost over time. It is the first essence to use to start your healing process.

There are flower essences that aid the healing of every conceivable emotional issue. There are essences that help heal the wounds from abuse and trauma, depression, anxiety, worry, procrastination, suicidal thoughts, selfishness, loneliness, histrionics, impatience, extreme materialism, low self-confidence and on and on and on. Therefore, you can also use flower essences to heal your own psychological issues, as well as helping you to be less susceptible to others' emotions. There is an important point I want to make in this regard.

If you are to truly gain control of your empathy, it is necessary to be aware of your own psychological issues. If you have been abused, react to stress with depression or anxiety, have very low self-esteem or other issues, it affects your empathic ability in the following way. We are most susceptible to the emotions we already have within us. If you are depressed, you will be most affected empathically by depression. You will sense depression and feel depressed emotions within you more easily than other types of painful emotions. The same goes for anxiety, anger and every other emotion. The reason behind this is no more complicated than the resonance of like energy.

It is simple, but it is a very important point. Although my chronic depression was primarily due to empathy, I always personally reacted to stressful situations with depression. That was what I naturally tended toward. I did not respond with anxiety, fear or panic. That was not my personality. I responded with depression. I now realize that while I was depressed, I was that much more vulnerable to empathically feeling other people's depression as well. It's a catch-22 that can be prevented by addressing your own psychological issues as much as possible.

The good news is that you will find it is much easier to finally heal those emotional problems that have plagued you all your life once you understand how empathy works. Since empathic people spend much of their lives feeling other people's emotions, it makes it extremely difficult to ever fully heal their own issues. There was always confusion as to what emotional pain was coming from within and what was being sensed from other people. With an understanding of empathy and using a flower essence like Yarrow, you will be able to identify much more clearly what are really your own issues. You'll have a much cleaner, straightforward emotional palette to work with, and you'll find that it will be much easier to heal and release old traumas and pains when empathic emotions are not constantly intruding.

It is perfectly all right to take more than one flower essence at a time. Many people like to take Yarrow along with a flower essence or two that directly relates to their own issues. This can result in some very profound healing. Let's revisit Janelle and Donnie from Chapter 2 to demonstrate how more than one flower essence can be used at a time.

Janelle

Remember Janelle from Chapter 2? She was the young, sensitive black female who overwhelmed her counselor because she had so many issues and complaints. She was a very emotionally sensitive person. She was easily hurt, upset and stressed. She was very self-conscious about a minor physical disability. Janelle was not coping well with problems at her job and with her new roommate. She was prone to anxiety, tension and panic. Janelle would often state she worried that something was wrong with her, and envied other people who seemed less sensitive and better able to cope with stress than she did.

Janelle decided to take three flower essences, Yarrow, Mimulus and Chamomile. She decided to take **Yarrow** because she was aware that she was an extremely sensitive person. Janelle exhibited every characteristic of emotional sensitivity. She was greatly impacted by other people's moods, and often felt uncomfortable and stressed around others. She took Yarrow to help rebalance her sensitivity and empathic ability, so that she would not feel so vulnerable and impacted by her surroundings.

Mimulus is a flower essence that helps heal anxiety and fear. Janelle generally met life's challenges with hesitation, anxiety and unease. She hoped Mimulus would allow her to experience greater courage and confidence, and help relieve her feelings of tension and anxiety. **Chamomile** is a flower essence that is described as helping people who are easily upset, moody and irritable, and have difficulty releasing emotional tension. That description matched Janelle to a "t," She experienced a lot of anxiety, but she also was moody, stressed and felt a constant undercurrent of anger and resentment. She was always upset about something and could never be happy. Chamomile essence seemed like a good choice to address her overall emotional style.

Since Janelle had so many emotional issues that all felt equally important, she took all three of these flower essences simultaneously. She began to notice beneficial effects after taking the essences for two weeks, but she continued taking them for a while afterward. Keep in mind that Janelle had felt very emotionally sensitive, anxious and moody for almost as long as she could remember. She had been to counseling without improvement and was at a loss as to what could ever make her situation better. In the face of all that, flower essences had an impact.

Janelle felt a release of physical tension so that her musculature was no longer so hard and tense. This made the limp from her physical disability slightly less noticeable, which pleased Janelle a great deal. She also felt a release of tension from her stomach area. She had never been aware that she was holding so much tension in her body. She felt less anxiety and fear, so she was able to remain calmer when faced with challenges. She began feeling less envious of others, and felt less affected by other people's moods. Overall she felt more comfortable with other people and more comfortable with herself.

Janelle did not instantly become the picture of happiness and contentment, but the level of her sensitivity, tension, anxiety and moodiness was reduced. Janelle stated she felt like she was "finally living like a regular person." She didn't have to be overwhelmed with negative emotions all the time. For the first time in years, Janelle was able to be around other people and have fun in group settings. Janelle has continued to use flower essences and has made even more progress since then. She has become much more comfortable with her sensitivity. Janelle is now beginning to understand how empathy played a part in her emotional suffering. She was always susceptible to taking on the negative emotions of those around her, but was quick to identify those painful emotions as her own problem and weaknesses. She is now able to discern between her own struggles and the emotions she senses from other people.

Donnie

Donnie was the 12-year-old boy we talked about in Chapter 2. He was a sensitive kid who was a quiet, good student. He didn't want to participate in after school activities, despite his parents' encouragement. He was often moody, but could not explain why. Donnie worried a lot about his father who suffered from depression.

Donnie's parents located a flower essence practitioner in their area who recommended two essences for Donnie, Pink Yarrow and Purple Monkeyflower. **Pink Yarrow** was recommended because Donnie was very worried about his father. He seemed to have such desire to help his father that he was empathically taking his father's depression into himself.

Donnie was not keen on the concept of empathy or psychic feeling. He was a bright kid from a traditional family who regularly attended Catholic church. Donnie was not comfortable with the concept of any kind of psychic ability, and was scared by the idea that he could feel other people's emotions. The flower essence practitioner inquired about this further and found out that Donnie frequently experienced nightmares and had a lot of fears about "spooky things he had seen and heard at night." The practitioner recommended Purple Monkeyflower essence to help calm Donnie's fears.

Purple Monkeyflower (*Mimulus kelloggii*) is a plant that is related to the Mimulus flower essence mentioned above in Janelle's case. Mimulus calms anxiety and fear. Since Purple Monkeyflower is a similar plant, it also calms fear, but is specific to the particular type of fear that Donnie expressed. Purple Monkeyflower addresses fear related to experiences of a spiritual or psychic nature. It helps people feel more secure and safe with their experiences, even though the experiences may not make sense from their conventional religious or intellectual viewpoint. It reduces the conflict between societal conventions and expectations versus the individual's personal experiences.

Donnie's father agreed to try taking flower essences for his depression. He was concerned that Donnie had been so affected by his depression, so he was willing to try a new remedy to prevent that from happening again in the future. The practitioner recommended **Mustard** flower essence for Dad. Mustard helps heal those who experience generalized depression without an obvious cause. They suffer from overwhelming gloom and despair. Mustard works by helping the depressed person come to terms with deep, unreconciled events from their past.

Donnie felt almost immediate relief from his flower essences. He didn't spend so much time and energy worrying about his father. He made a couple new friends who he liked to play with after school. Donnie's mother was pleased that he seemed happier and more energetic.

Dad stated that he felt like the Mustard flower essence was beneficial. It took the edge off his depression. Dad does not experience the extreme despair like he used to. He is now going to counseling and is ready to try other flower essences to promote further emotional healing. The entire family is grateful for the benefits flower essences had for them.

How to Use Flower Essences

The key to using flower essences correctly is to follow the directions on the bottle. Take the recommended small dose consistently. Increase the dosage by using the essence more frequently, not by taking a larger amount at a time. Taking a larger amount will not make a difference, and will only waste your essence you paid for. The recommended dosage of a small number of drops is completely sufficient. I mention this because a few tiny drops seem like such a small amount, people have the tendency to want to take more at a time. The recommended dosage varies slightly by brand. Trust the dosage that is given on the bottle. Flower essence makers have researched their products. The number of drops they recommend is the optimal amount to use.

From the case examples given above, you have read how a person can take one essence or a combination of essences at a time. The number of essences you take is up to you, but I encourage you to not go too hog wild. Compared to most health remedies, flower essences are fairly inexpensive. Add to that the fact that there are enough different flower essences to address just about every emotional issue there is, and you can see why people have a tendency to want to take a ton of essences at a time.

If you are choosing your essences by reading their descriptions in a book like this one or the descriptions from the manufacturer, then I recommend that you not take more than 3 or 4 essences at a time. Choose your essences to address your most broad-based, vexing emotional issues. Allow time for the essences to work. You'll probably find that they help you in unexpected ways, and that you don't need to buy as many flower essences as you had originally thought. This saves money and allows you to focus in on your issues and the process of your healing.

If you are choosing your essences with an intuitive technique, such as kinesiology, or if a flower essence practitioner is intuitively choosing essences for you, then it is acceptable to use more than 4 essences at a time. When essences are chosen by intuitive rather than purely intellectual methods, they are more likely to work synergistically and function together as a unit.

If you are interested in flower essences, then it will help you to read a book specifically about them. Good flower essence books explain how essences are made, the different methods of prescribing and taking flower essences, and how they work. Some flower essence books are listed in the Recommended Reading section of this book.

Flower Essences & Children

Flower essences are flexible remedies, which make them ideal for use with children. They should generally be taken 3 or 4 times per day, but they do not have to be taken at regimented times. So that means a child does not have to take them to school. If the child takes her essences before and after school and once or twice in the evening, that is satisfactory. Flower essences have no appreciable taste or smell for kids to complain about and no side effects for parents to worry about. Flower essence drops can be put in other types of beverages besides water, such as juice, for finicky kids.

Vibrational Essences

Flower essences fall under the heading of vibrational remedies. The term *vibrational* refers to the fact that the healing energy of the plant is transferred to the liquid remedy. Flower essences are a type of vibrational remedy. As you research essences and essence manufacturers, you will notice that there are more than just flower essences. Essences are also made from other parts of the plant as well as from things such as minerals and gemstones. All essences are made with basically the same approach and work in similar ways. Flower essences are currently the most popular and widely available vibrational essences, but don't ignore the other types of vibrational essences that may also be helpful for you.

The appendix in the back of this book lists numerous essence manufacturers and their contact information. Some of them make other types of essences in addition to flower essences. Look in the appendix to see how you can obtain the flower essences described in this chapter.

What's next?

Flower essences are the key to rebalancing and easing empathy. But we're still not done. So far we have gained knowledge about empathy and have learned how to heal and rebalance it. We have yet to learn how to control and manage empathy once it is rebalanced, or how to develop empathy positively. The next two chapters will address those issues, beginning in Chapter 5 with a lesson in visualization.

Chapter 5
Visualization & Meditation

Thus far in this book you have learned a tremendously new way of looking at your emotional sensitivity. Most sensitive people live their lives in varying degrees of emotional pain, without any understanding as to why. The cause of their sensitivity is a mystery, and they are at a loss as to how to relieve the emotional discomfort that is an everyday part of their lives. Those sensitive people who develop depression or anxiety are diagnosed with a mental disorder, and are convinced that something is horribly wrong with them. Millions of people across the world endure this emotional suffering solely because our society does not believe in empathic ability.

Now that you understand how empathy is at the root of sensitivity you have options that were never before available to you. By acknowledging your empathic ability, you open the door to true healing of the painful aspects of sensitivity. Chapter 4 presented flower essences, the means to heal empathic wounds that have accumulated over the years. Most all sensitive people will need to take this as the first step in regaining control of their empathic ability. You have to start by healing the pain that has accumulated over the years. Luckily, we have flower essences available as an effective means to accomplish this.

Flower essences heal our empathic ability in more ways than one. Not only can they help release painful emotions, but they also regulate our empathy. We suffered from the painful aspects of sensitivity because we had no idea how to control or manage our empathic ability. Flower essences can put you back on the right track. Taking an essence like Yarrow is, in effect, like pushing the reset button on your empathic ability. It gives you the opportunity to start fresh, with a balanced, protected feeling.

I am reviewing this topic because I want you to understand why I presented flower essences before other means of managing your empathic ability. I have repeatedly found that sensitive people benefit tremendously from flower essences. We have all suffered for years from lack of information about our empathy. The existence of empathic ability has been dismissed, denied and buried. Even though you may now be aware of your empathy, you are, unfortunately, not starting from a clean slate. You are becoming aware of your empathic ability after years of emotional distress, confusion and empathic distortion. Flower essences function to clear out and rebalance the distortion and confusion, so that you can reconnect with your empathy in a much clearer, more protected manner.

You will be able to tell when your empathic ability has been rebalanced. You will no longer feel so painfully sensitive. You will not be as agitated or overwhelmed by other people. You will feel like there is a natural boundary of protection around you that was missing for years. You will feel more capable and less vulnerable. You will realize that being sensitive does not mean you are doomed to always be overwhelmed or inundated by the world around you. Once you begin to feel this way, you will be ready to reconnect with your empathic ability.

That should make it clear why I feel flower essences are such an important resource for sensitive people. It would not be appropriate or useful to attempt to reconnect with your empathic ability when you are still in a state of overwhelm. Animosity and resentment toward your sensitivity would probably prevent you from making much beneficial progress. Plus it is very difficult to get a true sense of your empathy or how it works when you are still plagued by the painful aspects of sensitivity. That is why using flower essences to remove these barriers is the first step.

The next question to address is, "What is the point of reconnecting with your empathic ability?" Relieving the painful aspects of sensitivity and healing chronic depression may seem like enough of a goal. For most sensitive people, emotional relief is the only goal that has ever occurred to them. So why is there any need to go beyond that? Before we begin to discuss visualization and meditation, we need to answer that question.

The Empathic Sense

An important point to keep in mind is that your empathic ability is an integral part of who you are, and it always will be. If you are a sensitive person, that means you are strongly empathic. Nothing will change that. Now keep in mind that empathy is not a liability. It was frustrating, confusing and oftentimes painful when we were unaware of our empathic ability. But now that you are aware of it, the emotional pain can diminish and the frustration and confusion will begin a metamorphosis into curiosity about this ability you have. Empathic ability is another sense that is available to you. You have sight, smell, hearing, taste, and touch, and now you can also have within your control the ability to empathically sense emotional information.

Our five physical senses of sight, hearing, taste, touch and smell are all ways that we receive information about the world around us. People and the environment interact with us and communicate to us through our five senses. Empathy is also a form of communication with the world around us. Empathic ability is yet another type of sense, which provides us with information about our environment. Each of our senses reacts to stimuli that we often cannot directly observe. We hear the results of sound waves. We smell molecular compounds. With our empathic sense, we feel nonverbal emotional communication. We cannot physically see the stimulus that affects our empathic sense, but that is not much different from the molecules or sound waves that we also cannot directly see. The empathic sense may have been devalued by our culture, but it still exists. Along with your five physical senses, empathy goes about its business constantly receiving information about your environment.

Throughout this book, we have discussed how our empathic ability is affected by our society. A point to keep in mind is that the culture we live in shapes all of our senses, not just empathy. Our sense of taste is molded by the foods we eat as we grow up. Many adults find certain foods unpalatable simply because they were never exposed to them earlier in their life. Our sense of sight is greatly impacted by the activities we regularly engage in in our culture. Would so many of us be nearsighted or farsighted if we didn't spend countless hours with our eyes focused on reading, television, and computer monitors? Our senses are greatly affected by the world we live in. This is a fact of life, and in general we find this acceptable. You don't hear people complaining that their sense of taste or smell has been stunted by societal limitations of foods and aromas. Even the thought of a statement like that might seem silly, but consider this case in point.

Many of us suffer from distorted, blurred vision. It is an uncomfortable byproduct of the demands required in our society. How do we respond to this situation? We wear corrective lenses and don't give it much more thought. Does it ever occur to people to abandon their sense of sight because we have caused it to become distorted? Absolutely not, because we consider sight to be a source of vital information about our environment. Even if our sense of sight is not perfect, we can work around that in order to continue receiving the benefits of vision. Empathy is also a useful sense that should not be approached any differently. It is a sad fact, though, that most sensitive people wish they could get rid of their empathy because they regard it as a painful liability. These are the same people who would fight tooth and nail to preserve their vision or hearing, no matter how distorted those senses might become. This is because we never learned to value our empathic sense.

Empathic ability has been devalued by our society because it is not as tangible or intellectual as our physical senses, but that does not mean it is not useful. Empathy rounds out our senses by providing us with emotional information. When we interact with someone, we use all our senses to gather information about that person. This includes our empathic sense whether we have been aware of it or not. The depression, anxiety or anger we sensed and felt from other people were due to our empathic sense. The gut feelings that we often have about a person or a situation are also from our empathy.

This is the reason why it is necessary to reconnect with your empathic ability. Your empathic sense will continue picking up emotional information from the people and environment around you, just as it has your entire life. Empathic ability is a sense, just like our other five senses. Its job is to alert us to the information it receives from our environment. It will not stop doing its job, no matter how much we misunderstand it or may try to diminish it. It is in our best interest to learn how to understand the information it is giving us. We can do this by reconnecting with our empathic ability. When you are connected and more comfortable with your empathic sense, it ceases being a painful liability. You no longer confuse other people's painful emotions with your own. You can use the information from your empathic sense in a protected, useful way.

The primary means of connecting with your empathic ability are visualization and meditation. Empathy is an internal sense; therefore, an internal technique like meditation is required to access it. Our other senses such as vision, hearing and taste are physical, and are thus developed by outward, physical means. For example, wine connoisseurs refine their sense of taste by frequently sampling wines and paying close attention to what they taste. Within a relatively short amount of time, the person can easily perceive taste qualities of the wine that she would not have noticed when she first began drinking wine. Her sense of taste was developed and refined by regular practice and close attention. The same is required to develop your empathic sense.

The only difference between taste and empathy is that you are used to using your sense of taste. You are familiar with different kinds of tastes and what they mean, and you have been since you were a small child. This is not the case with your empathic sense. You have not been aware of it, so when you have perceived empathic information in the past, you have not known it was empathy, much less how to interpret its meaning. Empathic ability can be developed and refined with practice and attention just like the wine expert's sense of taste, but first you must know how to connect with your empathic sense.

If your goal is to become a wine authority, think how challenging it would be if you had never tasted wine before. You would have some catching up to do. That is the scenario that exists for most people in regard to their empathic sense. Development of empathy cannot begin until the empathic person is aware of her empathy and knows how to interpret the information it is conveying. Meditation allows you to connect with your empathic ability so you can better understand it and what it is trying to communicate to you.

Meditation

Let me first be clear about what I mean by meditation. Meditation is the practice of going within to connect with and pay attention to yourself. We spend our days externally focused. We interact with people, watch television, drive, run errands, and work. Our attention is on the outside world around us. We have thoughts that constantly chatter away in our minds that reflect this outward focus. We are usually thinking about the past, such as "What did my boss mean by that statement?" Or projecting into the future thinking about what's for dinner or our weekend plans. We spend very little time focused within ourselves or in the present moment.

Meditation is the practice of moving beyond the constant chatter of our thoughts to a quieter acceptance of yourself in the here and now.

For the purposes of this discussion the terms meditation, visualization, self-hypnosis, relaxation and imagery all refer to the same concept. The primary goal of all these similar practices is to move beyond the chatter of the mind and turn your focus inward, rather than outward as usual. It is well known that meditation promotes relaxation and benefits a person's physical and emotional well-being. Meditation is also the means for connecting with your empathic ability.

Practice Meditations

Five visualizations for practice are presented in the rest of this chapter. Read through them, and then decide which ones you want to practice with. This section applies to those who are practiced with meditation as well as those who have no experience at all. We'll begin with simple meditation basics, and progressively move up to visualization practices for connecting with your empathic sense. Please go through the meditations in the order presented. You will see how they teach you skills that build on each other up to the more advanced techniques for connecting with your empathic sense.

Our first relaxation session teaches you to turn your attention inward by focusing on the breath.

Breathing Meditation

Begin by sitting comfortably. Take a couple, slow deep breaths in through your nose and out through your mouth. Now readjust your body so that you are even more comfortable. Slow down your breathing a little more, very relaxed, in through your nose and out through your mouth.

Keep your breathing easy and soft. Notice how the air is cool as you inhale through your nose and warm as you exhale through your mouth. Pay attention to the coolness and warmth of the air for your next several breaths. Now notice how your chest and abdomen rise and fall with each breath. Allow your body to relax a little more. Let the chair or whatever you are sitting on fully support you. You do not have to exert any effort to sit there. Sink into the chair, releasing your muscles to feel heavy and relaxed. Take in a few deep, refreshing breaths. Listen for a few moments to the sounds around you. When you are ready, take in one more deep breath and exhale out your mouth.

That concludes this relaxation session.

This breathing meditation can be done with eyes closed or open. You can practice it at home alone, with your eyes closed, or with eyes open in public while you wait in line or during your lunch break. The hardest stumbling block most people encounter when learning to meditate is distracting thoughts. Our minds are used to racing with thoughts constantly. With this beginning relaxation, it really doesn't matter if you have some intruding thoughts. If you find yourself thinking about something and are no longer paying attention to your breath, just return your attention to your breathing and continue the meditation. With practice, distracting thoughts will interrupt less often.

The next meditation is longer and teaches you to focus your attention on your body, outside and in.

Body Meditation

Sit comfortably and take in a couple easy, deep breaths. Close your eyes and sit back relaxed and comfortable. Take in another slow, deep breath and relax into the chair, letting it support you. Begin by turning your attention to the top of your head. Focus your attention to your head. Feel the air as you breathe in and out through your nose. Can you feel your hair on your head, against your ears or neck? Allow your eyes to feel heavy and relaxed. Let your lips part slightly so your jaw relaxes.

Now let your attention drift downward to your torso and back. Pay attention to how your chest and abdomen rise and fall as you breathe. Notice the feeling of the chair against your back and legs. Let yourself sink deeper into the chair. Now notice your clothing. How does the material of your shirt feel against your skin, front and back? Continuing to notice your clothing, let your attention drift down to your legs. Feel the fabric against your legs, front and back. Eventually let your attention drift all the way down to your feet, and notice your socks or shoes.

Staying at your feet, turn your attention inward to inside your body. In your mind's eye visualize your skeleton and bones. Begin by visualizing the bones in your feet. Connect with those bones. How do they feel? See them clearly. Let your attention move up your legs. See and feel your anklebones and leg bones up to your knees. Notice the joints in your knees and your kneecaps. Let your attention continue to travel upward, noticing your thighbones and pelvis. Clearly see where your spine connects with the back of your pelvis. Travel up the spine, then follow your ribs around to the front. Visualize your collarbone, and let your attention fall down your arms. Feel the strength and solidity of the bones in your upper arms. Travel down to your elbow joints. Continue to see the bones of your lower arm, down to your hands and fingers. Clearly visualize the intricate bones in your hands.

Now turn your attention back to your spine. Follow your cervical spine up through your neck. Notice the vertebrae and how each one becomes just a little smaller as you get closer to your skull. Now visualize your skull. Let your attention go up over the top of your skull to the front bones of your face. Clearly see the front of your skull, down to your teeth and jaw.

Now get a mental picture of all the places you just visited, your entire skeleton. Feel your bones inside your body. When you're ready, turn your attention back to your breathing. Take in a deep breath. Feel your chest rise *and fall. Notice the sounds in the room around you. Take in one more deep, energizing breath and exhale. Open your eyes.*

That concludes this meditation.

This body-oriented meditation is a fun one for shifting your attention inward, quite literally. Since this visualization and the ones that follow are longer than the first one, you may want to record yourself or someone else slowly reading them. That way you can follow along with the tape, without having to try to remember what comes next. You can also visit my website at www.KyraMesich.com where I intend to have practice meditations available as audio files. The first two relaxation sessions presented so far prepare you for deeper meditation.

An exercise in visualization is next.

Forest Meditation

Close your eyes. Sit comfortably and take in several deep, relaxing breaths in through your nose and out through your mouth. Let each breath be just a little slower and a little deeper. Let yourself sink into the chair or whatever you are sitting on. Let your eyes feel heavy. Part your lips slightly so your jaw relaxes. Let your shoulders down, relaxed and heavy. Your entire torso feels heavy, completely supported by your chair. Allow the heavy feeling to flow down into your legs, all the way to your feet. Take in another slow, deep breath, and turn your attention to your mind's eye.

Picture in your mind that you are walking in a beautiful, serene forest. It can be whatever season you want, but the weather is perfect and you are protected and secure in your own private woods. Casually walk around for a bit to notice what you see. If it is day, where is the sun in the sky? What plants do you see around you? Are there any vistas where you can look out over the scenery?

Next notice what you hear. It may be the sound of the breeze rustling through the trees or squirrels scampering about. You may hear the calming babble of a nearby stream. Take a moment to notice what you hear in your ideal forest.

Pay attention to what you feel. You might notice the warmth of the sun on your skin or feel the breeze. Touch the rough bark of a big, old tree. Pick up a smooth stone and notice how different the sensations are between the bark and the stone.

Take in a deep breath of fresh, country air and notice how it smells. Feel free to bend down to sniff the perfume of a wildflower. Walk around for a bit longer and take in all the sights, sounds and experiences of your environment. This is your perfect, relaxing forest that can be however you wish. Know that you can return to this place whenever you like.

When you are ready to leave, return your attention to your breathing. Take a couple energizing breaths. Listen to the sounds in the room around you. Open your eyes.

That concludes this meditation.

This visualization teaches you the key to deep, successful meditation—using all of your physical senses. The word *visualization* implies only sight, and that is the biggest mistake that limits most people when they attempt to visualize. They only see a picture in their mind and nothing else. Think how limited and less satisfying your forest would have been if you had only looked at it. The addition of hearing, touching and feeling makes it much more real, and creates a far deeper, more relaxing meditation. If you can do this forest meditation using the varied senses as described above, then you will be way ahead of most people who are learning to meditate.

You can practice your visualization skills using any environment you want. You might find it more relaxing and fun to visualize a beach, your ideal dream home, a cloud in the sky, or anything else your imagination can come up with. Wherever you go in your meditation, just remember to use all your physical senses while you are there. You can incorporate taste by having a drink or snack in your ideal environment.

The forest visualization teaches you how to access your senses during meditation. Most people are surprised at how easy it is to connect with their senses in this way. They can clearly see the forest, hear the rustling leaves, smell the freshness of the air and flowers, and feel the tree bark. Your senses are always available for access when you focus inward during meditation. This is also true of your empathic sense.

The next meditation is a visualization for connecting with your empathic ability.

Comfortable Room Meditation

Sit comfortably with eyes closed, and take in a couple easy, deep breaths. Let yourself be fully supported by the chair or whatever you are sitting on. Take another slow breath, in through your nose and out through your mouth, and relax a little more. Let your head and neck relax, feeling heavy. Part your lips slightly, relaxing your jaw. Let your arms feel very heavy. The weight of your arms pulls down your shoulders, relaxing your back and torso. The heavy relaxation travels down to your thighs, down your legs, all the way to your feet. Take another slow, easy breath, and turn your attention to your mind's eye.

See yourself sitting in a very comfortable chair in a pleasant, protected room. You are very relaxed and secure in this room. Notice how it feels in the soft, supremely comfortable chair. The temperature in this room is exactly as you like it. You can fill this room with soft, comforting sounds or aromas if you like. This is your comfortable, secure room where you can come to rest and connect with your empathic sense.

The color of the walls in this room are changeable to reflect how you are feeling. What color is the room right now? How does that relate to your current emotions? Experiment with changing the color of the room. Think of a person you know. The color of the room may change. How does this color relate to your feelings about the person? Now think about an event that happened to you recently. Allow time for the room color to adjust. How does this color reflect your feelings about that event?

Now return your attention to the comfort and relaxation of your room, and allow the color to adjust as you rest comfortably in your chair. In this protected, comfortable place you can connect with your emotions and with your empathic sense at any time. All you have to do is request to be connected with your empathic sense. Do this now in your private room. Aloud or to yourself say, "I request to be connected with my empathic sense." Sit quietly for a moment and notice how it feels to connect with your empathy.

Ask your empathic sense to change the color of the walls to the color that is most important for you to see right now. Allow the color to change. What color have the walls changed to? How does it feel in the room now? What does this color mean to you? What is your empathic sense telling you with this color?

Take a deep breath, and take note once again of the color your empathic sense presented to you. Take a couple deep, energizing breaths. Know that you can come back to this room whenever you want to rest and connect with your empathic sense.

Now turn your attention back to your body. Feel your chest rise and fall as you breathe. Notice the sounds around you. Take in an energizing breath and exhale. When you are ready, open your eyes.

That concludes this meditation.

There is a lot involved in this visualization. Just like the forest meditation, you are creating a safe, calm environment in your mind's eye. The difference in this one is that you are creating a space where you can connect with your empathic sense as well as your physical senses. This is a very powerful meditation because it may be the first time you have connected with your empathic sense in any way. When you are ready to try this meditation, make sure you have enough time set aside and will not be disturbed. This is an important meditation that sets the stage for deeper understanding of your empathic ability.

The next visualization takes place in the same comfortable room where you will learn how to feel more protected and secure with your empathic sense.

Protection Meditation

Sit comfortably with your eyes closed, and take in a couple easy, deep breaths. Let yourself be fully supported by the chair or whatever you are sitting on. Take another slow breath, in through your nose and out through your mouth, and relax a little more. Let your head and neck relax, feeling heavy. Part your lips slightly, relaxing your jaw. Let your arms feel very heavy. The weight of your arms pulls down your shoulders, relaxing your back and torso. The heavy relaxation travels down to your thighs, down your legs, all the way to your feet. Take another slow, easy breath, and turn your attention to your mind's eye.

See yourself sitting in a very comfortable chair, in a pleasant, protected room. This is the colorful room where you connect with your empathic sense. You are very relaxed and secure in this room. Notice how it feels in the soft, comfortable chair. The temperature in this room is exactly as you like it. You can fill this room with soft, comforting sounds or aromas if you like. This is your comfortable, secure room where you come to rest and con-nect with your empathic ability.

Ask to be connected with your empathic sense. Sit quietly for a moment and notice how it feels to be connected with your empathy. This time you are going to ask your empathy to change the color of the room to a safe, protective color that you can use to safeguard your empathic ability from other people's painful emotions. Ask your empathic sense to show you a color that will protect it from taking in too much negativity. Allow time for the color of the walls to change.

How does this color feel to you? Does it feel like a strong, protective color? Are you comfortable with this color? If not, ask your empathy to show you another color until you are comfortable. Feel how this color is strong, secure and protective. You are going to use this color to create a protective shield for your empathic ability.

Picture a field of energy that surrounds you like a sphere, extending out all around you. It extends above your head and below your feet. It goes down into the chair you are sitting in, and extends out in front of you. Now let this sphere of energy become the protective color of the room.

This is a strong field of energy that protects you and your empathy from unwanted negative emotions. See the field of energy infused with the protective color. How does this energy feel around you? Sit and notice for a moment how it feels to have this protective energy around you. You can call on this energy and the protective color at any time to shield you from other people's emotions.

Now turn your attention to your breathing and your body. Feel your chest rise and fall as you breathe in and exhale. Notice that the protective energy is still with you. Take a couple more deep, energizing breaths. Hear the sounds around you. Remember that the protective energy and color are always available to you, no matter where you are. You can call upon them at any time to shield your empathic sense from taking in too much negativity. Take in one more deep breath and exhale. When you are ready, open your eyes.

That concludes this visualization.

This meditation supplies you with a tool you can use anytime to shield your empathic sense from taking in too much painful emotion. You don't have to go through the entire meditation every time. When you feel the need for empathic protection at work or in a busy, crowded place, quickly visualize the protective color and energy around you. You will get better at it, and it will work more effectively the more you practice.

That was the last visualization for this chapter. As you have read, the meditations progressed through learning to focus attention, focus inward, how to connect with your physical senses during meditation, and a meditative technique for connecting with your empathic sense. If you don't have much experience with meditation, take your time as you progress through these visualizations. Begin with the first breathing meditation and practice until you feel comfortable with it. When you are ready, start practicing the next one. Don't rush yourself through these meditations because you are learning skills that build on each other. It is important that you feel proficient with each meditation before you move on to the next one.

Troubleshooting

It is not unusual for people to complain that they cannot successfully meditate. They say that no matter what they do, no matter how much they practice, they cannot focus their attention for very long. Distracting thoughts always intervene. It is a fairly common problem. Keep in mind that it will be easier to do the longer meditations if you have them recorded. Your mind can relax more easily if you are following along with a recording, rather than trying to remember a long meditation yourself.

The forest visualization is a wonderful meditation for learning to focus attention and quiet the mind. Using all the physical senses during meditation greatly reduces the problem of distracting thoughts. If you find that you still can't focus your attention even after practicing the forest visualization, then there are a couple possibilities for what might need to be addressed.

Take stock of the current stressors in your life. If you are very stressed at work, are having relationship problems, or are going through any kind of difficulty that is very stressful for you, it will interfere with your ability to meditate. It may seem ironic that you can't meditate at the time when you really need to relax, but that is the way it is. If you are very stressed, upset, or going through a crisis, your mind will not be able to let go enough for you to effectively meditate. Once the crisis passes, you will be able to focus your attention much more easily.

Another even more common scenario that interferes with meditation relates not to present stressors, but to ones from the past.

In order to turn your attention inward and meditate deeply it is vital to feel safe and secure. If you do not feel safe, on any level, you will not be able to meditate deeply. Your mind will jump in and interrupt the process. Many of us do not feel safe at our core because of childhood pain. If you were abused sexually, physically or emotionally, or if you grew up in a family in which you did not feel protected, you compensated for that early in your life by putting up emotional defenses and intellectual barriers. These old defenses kick in during meditation when you are trying to relax and focus inward. Your defenses think that you need to be on guard 100% of the time. They aren't interested in looking inward, where the realm of the psyche and emotions are. So, unfortunately, the defenses that helped you survive a hostile environment as a child only serve to hurt you as an adult. They keep you from ever being able to truly relax or connect with yourself.

These old defenses can be unlearned and overcome. Refer to my e-book *Modern Meditation* (visit **www.KyraMesich.com** for ordering information) for further discussion of this topic and healing methods for restoring a sense of protection and safety. An ironic point I need to mention here is that highly empathic people often feel unprotected at their core because their empathy has been exposed to so much emotional pain over the years. You may have developed protective defenses in attempt to deal with your empathic sense, which you didn't understand at the time. Learning about empathic ability and taking the flower essences recommended in Chapter 4 should restore an inner sense of protection so you can meditate successfully.

This chapter introduced the concept that empathic ability is actually another sense, just like our five physical senses. The problem is that the empathic sense has been devalued and misunderstood by our society. It is important to learn to reconnect with your empathic sense because it continually receives and conveys information about our environment just like our other senses of vision, hearing, taste, touch and smell. Until we reconnect with our empathic sense, it is very difficult to interpret the information it is trying to relay to us. Meditation provides the means for connecting with our empathy.

Empathic ability is a skill that provides you with very useful information not normally available to your intellect. Thus far in this book you have learned how to rebalance your empathy and how to reconnect with it, so you are no longer susceptible to the painful aspects of sensitivity. The next chapter finally gets to the fun part, developing your empathy so that it works for your benefit. Chapter 6 takes you to the next step, learning to develop and refine your empathic ability, so that you can truly understand and profit from the information it provides.

Chapter 6
Positive Development of Empathy

Empathic ability is a very useful skill. It provides you with information about people and your environment that you would have no access to intellectually. Our empathic sense would be naturally balanced and protected like all of our other senses if we had learned about it as we were growing up. Unfortunately, since our culture devalues and denies the existence of empathy, we were left confused, suffering from a myriad of painful emotional symptoms.

Nightmares

For years I was haunted by horribly violent dreams. I was chased or attacked by a murderous villain nearly every night. The settings of the nightmares varied. One night it would be in a dark alley, the next a labyrinth like mansion, sometimes it was simply in an open field. But the theme remained constant. I had to defend myself against my attacker, to fight or die an unpleasant and scary death. So in every dream I chose to fight, with graphic, violent, bloody results. But at least I always won.

These dreams recurred for years. I could never make sense of them. Why was I plagued by such violent images? My subconscious was intent on these scenes of mortal danger. Why did it think I needed to fight for my life? I didn't have a clue, and I found the graphically violent images quite disturbing. This is one of those kinds of symptoms that doesn't make the slightest bit of sense from an intellectual perspective. My dreams could have been analyzed up and down by the world's greatest therapists, and no one would ever have interpreted their intended message correctly.

People search for the symbolic meaning in dreams. They look for archetypes and assume that it is in the foreign language of the subconscious, which has to be translated before it can be understood. But in the case of my dreams, the meaning was flat out literal. I was under attack. I did need to fight back and defend myself, and it was, in fact, a matter of life or death.

My empathic sense was so inundated, I was pierced by painful emotions all the time. Intellectually, I had just about given up. As far as I could tell, I was doomed to suffer from emotional pain and depression my entire life. My view of the future was matter of fact. I figured that eventually the day would come when I would be so worn down I would no longer be able to resist the suicidal urges I so frequently felt, and that would be that. My dreams were screaming to me that I was being bombarded, and that I had to do something about it. They were trying to show me that I had the strength, ability and resources to fight for my life and win. And they were right.

Intuition

In the years since those dreams, I have rebalanced and reconnected with my empathy so that it is no longer a source of pain. I no longer suffer from chronic depression. The dreams haven't recurred because I finally got the message. My life has turned around 180 degrees, all because I now understand my empathic ability and have been willing to heal and develop it. I now realize that empathy is an important, integral feature of who I am. The symptoms of depression and the painful aspects of emotional sensitivity were not due to empathy itself. They were caused by the *disconnection* from my empathic ability.

Reconnection with my empathic ability led to complete symptom relief, but that is not where the story ends. Since then I've realized that empathy is an amazingly beneficial and useful ability. Reconnection with our empathic sense leads to profound healing on all levels, yet this is not where you should stop. It is not just a matter of healing the pain that was created by our overwhelmed empathy. The potential of reconnection with our empathic ability goes far beyond healing old wounds. The next step is reclaiming this natural empathic ability that we all have in its entirety.

Empathic ability is much more than emotional communication, as we would define it from our narrow intellectual viewpoint. Empathy is emotional communication as I have stated throughout this book, but what I have come to understand is that emotional communication encompasses the vastness of everything that is not of the intellect. That is a huge realm, and it is all accessible through our empathic ability.

To put it very simply, empathy is the same thing as intuition. It provides us with information that cannot be received by the intellectual mind. The easiest way to explain what I mean by this is to share the steps I went through in the development of my own empathic ability.

Steve

The refinement of my empathic ability began after the initial stages of healing with flower essences and visualization. Eventually I got to the point where my empathy was becoming rebalanced. I was no longer being inundated by emotions. I no longer felt vulnerable or afraid I would be impacted by other people's pain. As the healing process continued, I received a couple demonstrations of the positive potential empathy holds.

I was enrolled in an acting class, which took place in the basement of a local theatre. At first the classes were fun. I was enjoying the process of learning some new, useful techniques. A few weeks in, the instructor announced that she wouldn't be teaching anymore due to schedule conflicts, so a new instructor named Steve would be taking over. I didn't feel bad about this news at the time. I had learned a lot from the first instructor, but it could also be good to get a different perspective from another teacher. I could potentially be getting more for my money.

The next session started with Steve taking a considerable amount of time to introduce himself. He was a dark haired, striking man who had worked for many years as a professional actor. As I sat there, surrounded by my classmates who were listening attentively, I had a funny feeling about Steve. I couldn't say I didn't like him. I hadn't even interacted with him yet. I couldn't identify anything about his mannerisms or what he was saying that was turning me off. Nonetheless, I had a distinct feeling in my gut that I needed to be wary around this man.

Steve was an enthusiastic and involved instructor. He gave individual attention and feedback to all the students in the class. He was charming, witty and entertained us with funny stories of behind-the-scenes Hollywood from his television acting days. He had won over his students completely. Everyone thought he was great. Intellectually, I should have been as enthralled with him as everyone else. There was no objective reason to feel anything less. Nonetheless, my situation only became more confusing as the weeks passed. I couldn't ignore my gut feelings, which got progressively more intense. I sensed that Steve was controlling and egotistical. Whenever I was around him, my gut was constantly and loudly prodding me that something was up with this guy, and I shouldn't trust him.

The worst part of it was not the gut feeling itself, but that all my classmates loved Steve. After classes they would talk about how great they thought he was, which left me absolutely baffled. Why did I feel so differently? And most importantly, why was I the only one? I wondered what issues within myself were prompting my seemingly unusual reaction to Steve.

I had paid for an entire session of classes, so I intended to go to all of them, no matter what I felt about Steve. I reasoned that I should be able to continue learning in the classes if I maintained some emotional distance. It was a good plan, but it didn't work. My feelings about Steve got stronger and stronger with each class, until I had developed an outright contempt for him. I was confused by my feelings and felt completely alone. None of my classmates had changed their opinions. Instead, it seemed like their adoration of him grew in proportion to my disdain. The final straw came in the form of an unusual experience.

The classes were held at night. I was so beat on one particular night that by the time I drove back home I was ready to go straight to bed. I got into bed and pulled up the covers all nice and cozy, ready to drift off to restful slumber. Instead, a flash image of Steve suddenly hit me. It was accompanied by the feelings that he had emotionally attached himself to me, that he wanted something from me, and that he was trying to size me up to see if he could get whatever it was he wanted. This was a creepy and annoying experience. It was very intense, and seriously disrupted the mood for going to sleep after that.

I decided that was it. I couldn't attend his classes anymore. There were only a couple classes left in the session anyway, so it wasn't a huge monetary loss. I told a few of my classmates whom I had befriended that I wouldn't be in class anymore because I couldn't stand Steve and didn't trust him. Their mystified response was as I had expected. They didn't feel that way about him at all. A few of them said they were planning to sign up for his classes again the next session. I wished them good luck and said my goodbyes.

I couldn't make much sense of my feelings in regard to Steve. The fact that everyone else loved him made me doubt myself. But in the end, I had to admit that my feelings were so strong, I needed to heed them whether they made sense or not. My feelings were not like the empathic experiences I had had in the past. I wasn't feeling Steve's emotions. I had my own feelings about him, toward him. I also sensed that he had some kind of bad intentions, and I didn't care to find out firsthand what they were.

At the time I didn't think I would ever be able to make sense of why I felt so strongly toward Steve. I wasn't sure if this experience was due to empathy or not. All I knew was that I had to get away from Steve. That was the most important thing. I am very grateful that a couple months later I received information that helped me verify and understand the reasons for my reaction to Steve. One evening my phone rang. I picked it up, and the first words I heard were, "You were right about Steve."

The caller was one of my former classmates. She called to tell me what I had missed over the past couple months. As it turned out, Steve had set his sights on every one of his female students. In turn, he romanced and seduced each one of them, even though he was involved with another woman, living in her home. Obviously, he had tired of that relationship. He had a goal. He wanted a new place to live, so he was looking for a new woman who would let him move in to her place. The classmate who called me was horrified that she had nearly fallen for his scheme. She realized just in the nick of time that this was a pattern for him. To put it bluntly, he was a leech searching for a new host to bleed dry.

When I hung up from that phone call, I was relieved to know that my feelings had some basis in reality. My emotional response to Steve was inexplicable at the time. He had never done anything to me. I had no reason to dislike him or mistrust him. I had no way of knowing what his intentions were. Yet somehow I did. From this experience I learned that my gut feelings are a reliable source of information, and

I should trust them, no matter how much they might conflict with prevailing opinion.

I felt sure that these gut feelings had to be an aspect of empathic ability. Was this the sort of useful information empathy was intended to convey? I decided I would pay closer attention to gut feelings in the future. When and how do they come up? How does this type of empathic information differ from intellectual thoughts, such as forming an opinion about someone? I needed to wait for it to happen again, so I could learn more about it. I didn't have to wait very long.

Randy

My husband and I were involved in another theatre production. This time it was a silly slapstick comedy with a large cast. Following one of the first rehearsals, we all went out for coffee afterwards to get to know each other. We were a diverse group of people, ranging from teenagers to retirement-aged folks. We each told a little bit about ourselves, sharing information such as day job and where we grew up. Some people, of course, divulged more than others.

Randy was one of the biggest talkers. He was an older man who had just retired from his job as a public administrator. He regaled us with amusing stories about goof-ups in city politics. He wanted everyone to know that now that he was retired, he was focusing his attention on the artistic endeavors he had always wanted to do such as acting and writing.

On the drive home, my husband and I reviewed the events of the evening's rehearsal and our thoughts about our fellow actors. My husband mentioned Randy in particular. Randy had some humorous stories and seemed like an interesting fellow who might be entertaining to work with. I responded, "I don't know. I have a funny feeling about him."

I paid attention to my funny feeling, but it never became much more than that. Over the course of the first several rehearsals, my funny feeling remained constantly subtle, yet distinct. It was a small, gut feeling of wariness toward Randy. If I hadn't been specifically paying attention to my gut feelings, it would have been very easy to overlook. In the beginning, Randy was an amiable fellow who seemed dedicated to the show. There wasn't any outward reason for me to dislike him. Then, about halfway through rehearsals, his true character reared its ugly head.

Randy suddenly became the biggest prima donna in the history of community theatre. He complained about the quality of the props. He stormed out of rehearsals in a huff. He demanded extra attention to every small detail of his costumes, his props, and everything regarding his character. Working with him was a nightmare. He ruined the fun mood of our cast and our show. Yet all I ever felt about Randy was a small, funny feeling. My empathic warning didn't seem quite proportional to the amount of trouble he caused.

The quality of the empathic information was different this time from the gut feelings I had previously experienced in regard to Steve, the acting instructor. My gut feelings about both Steve and Randy had been accurate, but my experience of them seemed to represent the opposite ends of the scale. My feelings about Steve were extremely intense, with some pretty specific information. While, on the other hand, my empathic feelings about Randy were so subtle and vague, they could have easily been overlooked or dismissed. This left me with quite a few ideas to ponder.

First of all, how could I get in synch with my empathy so that the information I received from it would be more balanced? It would be ideal to experience empathic gut feelings at a medium sort of intensity, so it wouldn't be overwhelming, but would provide the needed information. I reasoned that this probably would evolve naturally over time as I paid attention to the development of my empathic ability. This was a new skill I was developing, it wouldn't be perfect from the start. Even more importantly, I wondered how I could be able access this useful empathic information at will.

The gut feelings I had about Steve and Randy were spontaneous. I wasn't trying to figure anything out about them. The information came to me out of the blue. I thought about how useful it would be to be able to purposely, at will, tap into empathy. How many times do we wish we had a clue about the true character or intentions of another person? Can I trust this person to take care of my house while I'm away on vacation? Will this real estate agent do the best job of selling my house? Which banker should I go to for my business loan? Should I go out on a date with this person?

Consider how much time and energy we put into fretting and going back and forth in our minds over these types of questions. And how many times we wish we would have made different choices. With an empathic approach, that process would be changed dramatically. We could simply tune into our empathic ability, ask the question regarding the other person, and receive a reliable, useful answer. So the question is, how can we tune into our empathic ability to hear what it has to say? I'm glad to report that the answer is a lot easier than you might think.

While browsing through the bookstore one evening, I was drawn to a small paperback titled *You Are Psychic!* by Pete A. Sanders. One lone copy of it was wedged in the middle of a shelf crammed with hundreds of books, yet for some reason it caught my attention. My goal that evening was part of my continual search to find books containing references to empathic ability. I had come up with nothing so far that evening, and I was getting tired. But I figured I had time to leaf through this one last book before I went home. As it turned out, this unassuming paperback contained a practical and clear method for learning how to tap into empathic information. It was exactly what I had been looking for.

The author, Pete Sanders, is an MIT-trained scientist who studied neurology and biomedical chemistry. His book is a culmination of years of research of psychic abilities. As the title of his book *You Are Psychic!* implies, Sanders has consistently found that everyone has the ability to develop psychic awareness. We all naturally possess psychic abilities, such as empathy, but most of us are unaware of it and have no idea how to control it or use it. Sanders uses the term *psychic feeling* to refer to empathy. It is exactly the same concept as empathic ability, just different words. Sanders' research findings correlate with what I have read from varied sources in regard empathic ability. The key to developing empathic ability is an area of the body called the solar plexus.

The Solar Plexus

An anatomical definition of the solar plexus is: a nerve plexus in the abdomen distributing nerve fibers to the viscera of the body. What this means in plainer language is that we have a complex, interlacing network of nerves located in the abdomen, which someone decided to name the solar plexus. This plexus of nerve fibers has direct connections to all our internal organs. It appears to be a primary communication point within our nervous system. The solar plexus is a major reception and switching station for nerve impulses. Since this specific network of nerves receives so much of the stimuli we encounter, it makes sense that it is the place where empathic information is processed. It also makes sense because we naturally associate the abdominal area with the realm of emotion and empathy.

Our language is filled with descriptions that connect the stomach area with emotional experiences. We have "gut feelings," feelings in "the pit of the stomach," and "butterflies in the stomach." The abdominal area of our body is a center for receiving, processing and responding to emotional stimuli. Tapping into this area to connect with empathic information is as simple as focusing attention toward the solar plexus.

To tune into the solar plexus, focus your attention to the area of your body between your chest and the belly. This abdominal area is the seat of the solar plexus. To connect with your empathic ability, all you have to do is focus your attention to the solar plexus and pay attention to what you feel there. When I first tried this method, I was amazed at how simple yet effective it is. But it goes to show that empathy is not a complex skill that is difficult to obtain. It is a natural ability that is not hard to use once we have recovered from the years of neglect and misunderstanding regarding empathic ability.

We are used to thinking in our heads. That is where we talk to ourselves, ponder questions, and figure out the answers. Our inner voice in our heads chatters away perpetually. Our constant thinking is the only obstacle in learning to connect with empathy. The challenge is to maintain focus on the solar plexus, and not let your attention drift back up to thoughts in your head. Here's a quick demonstration.

Notice right now where the activity is in your head as you are reading this book. It's somewhere up there between your ears. That is the same place where you think to yourself. Think to yourself for a moment and really notice where the inner words seem to be coming from. Where in your head is that inner dialogue taking place?

Now turn your attention to the solar plexus area (between you chest and your belly) and recall an emotional experience you had recently, such as watching a hilarious or sad movie, having fun at a party, or being scared by a sudden, loud noise. Once you have chosen your emotional experience to recall, pay attention to just the solar plexus area. Where do you feel that emotion? That is the exact location where you can focus to tune into your empathic ability.

When I began using this method to tune into empathy, there was gradual development with practice. At first I could easily sense the emotional impression in my solar plexus. Let's use the example of a common question, "Should I go to this party? Would it be a good experience for me to go?" Early in my empathic development, I could sense the emotional answer in my solar plexus. I would either get a happy, secure feeling that I should go, or sometimes I would feel an uneasy, knot in the stomach that meant I would be much better off doing something else instead of the party.

With practice, I have developed my empathic ability so that the answers I receive are much more complete. I can direct my attention toward my solar plexus, ask a question, and receive a fairly detailed empathic answer, which includes feelings as well as concepts. Now when I ask, "Should I go to this party?" The response will contain a feeling, like the positive, secure feeling, as well as the reason behind the positive answer such as, "You are afraid that you won't know anyone at this party, but you will meet some fun people. It would be in your best interest to go." Or if the response I receive is simply a positive "yes," I can ask, "Why?" I'll then receive further explanation such as, "Someone will be at that party who knows about book publishing. It would be helpful for you to meet her." Empathic information feels as natural as the thoughts I think to myself all the time, but they are centered in the solar plexus area, not up in my head.

So how can you do this for yourself? How can you get where I am to be able to easily connect with your empathic ability and derive the useful benefits it provides? The first step is not to jump the gun too much. Before anything else, you have to heal the depression and other psychological symptoms that were a result of unawareness of empathy. Once those problems are no longer plaguing you, you'll be able to move forward in a healthier way.

Keep in mind that empathy is emotional communication. It was not intended to be painful or to be confused with our own emotions. It was intended to provide us with emotional information about the world around us. It is very useful to understand what another person is feeling when you have to live, work or otherwise interact with that person. It greatly enhances and smoothes relationships when people can communicate on an emotional level. Once your empathy is balanced and healed, you will be aware of other people's emotional states without taking the emotions within yourself. You will be aware, in a protected manner.

Once you are more secure and protected and feel like you have reconnected with your empathic ability, the only requirement is patience and willingness to devote the time to develop your empathic ability to its full, intended potential.

Since we are such a goal-oriented society, the question that always comes from this is, "What is the highest, ultimate development of empathy?" "What is the goal we're reaching for?" I do have the answer, which might not be quite what you were thinking. The ultimate development of empathy is, simply put, reconnection with yourself. The goal is reunification of all aspects of yourself. We are not whole when we are disconnected from our empathic ability. That is why we were vulnerable, confused, and in pain. It is far easier to be a happy, contended, productive, successful person when you are integrated. You can better understand and communicate with yourself, as well as relate with other people.

Empathy is emotional communication between people, but also communication within yourself. We all wonder why we do certain things. Why do I keep getting involved in destructive relationships? Why am I procrastinating so much on this project? Why do I feel so tense? When we aren't tuned in to our empathic ability, we don't know how communicate with ourselves to hear the straight answers to these kinds of questions. Empathy allows you to communicate with yourself, so you can understand the reasons behind your behavior and better solve your problems.

Developing empathic ability is a rewarding process that improves your life from within. People are clambering these days to learn how to develop their intuition, not realizing that empathy is already an innate part of who they are. With some straightforward guidance and practice, you can develop your empathic ability to whatever level you wish. To aid your practice, I recommend that you obtain a copy of the book *You Are Psychic!* by Pete Sanders. It contains simple exercises for developing psychic feeling as well as other intuitive abilities. As you progress with the development of your empathic ability, you'll come to realize how limiting and unbalanced it was to rely solely on intellect for information about yourself and the world around you.

We have covered a lot of ground in these chapters. The reason I wrote this book was so people would know that there is a basis for their emotional sensitivity and recurrent depression. Empathic ability is the underlying cause of depression and emotional suffering much more commonly than one might think. Everyone is born with an empathic sense. Due to the culture we live in, some people's empathic ability fades with time, but this is not the case for highly empathic people. Their empathy continues sensing other people's emotions until it becomes overwhelmed. This empathic distortion is the cause of many people's chronic depression. This is a radically new explanation for psychological symptoms.

It is unfortunate that empathic ability is seen as a radical, unusual explanation for emotional distress because it is in fact very common. Empathic ability is the underlying cause of emotional sensitivity. Sensitive people's emotional discomfort and overwhelm are explained by empathic ability. People need not suffer from the painful aspects of sensitivity once they realize that empathy is the cause. Common thought dictates that emotionally sensitive people are weak, emotionally fragile and doomed to suffer from psychological symptoms and emotional overwhelm. These ideas are wrong. When sensitive people reconnect with their empathic sense, they can be released from the emotional discomfort that seemed never-ending.

Empathic ability often manifests as the experience of literally feeling another person's emotions as if they were your own feelings. This is not the way empathy was intended to work. Empathy becomes distorted over our lives because we have no knowledge of it, and no way to interpret the empathic feelings we sense. Over time, our empathic sense becomes more and more overwhelmed until the emotional pain finally seizes our attention. Sadly, our intellectual mind interprets this emotional pain as faults and weaknesses stemming from our own psyche, rather than empathic information coming from outside ourselves.

Empathy is intended to be pure emotional communication from a safe, protected vantage. Our empathic sense is designed to provide us with information about people and our environment beyond the limits of our intellect and physical senses. You can rebalance and reconnect with your empathic ability and restore its functioning to the healthy, beneficial manner in which it should be. This not only relieves lifelong psychological symptoms, but also opens the door to connecting with your intuition.

Despite its prevalence, empathic ability has been a taboo subject for hundreds of years. It's not easy to overcome that with one book. Nevertheless, I have confidence that the reality of empathic ability will be accepted. It is part of who we are as human beings. Denying, ignoring or diminishing empathic ability does not make it go away. It only causes it to manifest in ways that cause pain and discomfort, which finally force us to stop and take notice that it is there. Empathic ability is our direct connection to emotion and intuition. It is the basis of our humanity. Just because empathy has been tossed aside in favor of the physical and intellectual does not mean that it won't be reclaimed. The time is now right for people to understand this aspect of themselves that has been there all along.

Thank you for taking the time to read this book on what some would deem a controversial subject. In fact, empathic ability is such a misunderstood concept that there were many obstacles to this book's publication. Hopefully, in time, empathic ability will be regarded as a familiar skill we all possess, and people will no longer suffer from the pain that results when we are cut off from a vital part of who we are.

Epilogue

A Message for Counselors, Therapists and All Helping & Healing Professionals

This note is especially for those who work in the helping and healing professions: nurses, psychologists, counselors, massage therapists, social workers, chiropractors, doctors, energy healers, home health care providers, personal coaches, crisis workers, etc.

Sensitive people often find themselves drawn to these types of professions. This makes sense because empathic people are naturally skilled at understanding and helping other people. However, it is also ironic. By working in this type of job, the empathic person exposes herself to a continually intense emotional environment.

This is why it is often in the workplace where sensitive people realize just how empathic they are. Many sensitive healers find themselves periodically overwhelmed or drained by their clients' emotions. Sadly, though, these professionals suffer in silence because it puts one's job and professional reputation in jeopardy to admit to feeling overwhelmed. Intellectually, we are not supposed to allow that to happen. Our training and our dedication to our work is supposed to supply us with all the tools we need to function perfectly in our respective jobs. This is the myth of almost all training programs in the health field.

Far too few schools address the healer's personal needs for protection and boundaries. This leaves therapists and healers extremely vulnerable to the intense emotional energy that pervades their work environment everyday. The underlying belief most of us have when we set out to begin our healing careers is that we will be expected to deal with extreme emotions constantly, and that it should not have a significant impact on us personally. Read this statement one more time and note how absurd it actually is. We will interact with pained, distressed people constantly, yet it will have no impact upon us whatsoever. As preposterous as this notion is, it is nonetheless the belief system that almost all of us carry into our jobs. We blindly accept that somehow we are supposed to be caring, nurturing, giving and helpful while simultaneously impervious to the emotions and energies of our clients.

This is why it is nothing short of alarming for the sensitive healer to have the realization that his patients are affecting him. How can you maintain the expected objective, professional distance when you are personally experiencing your client's distress? It doesn't get any more intimate than that. Your emotions influenced by another person's energy, beyond your control. Subconscious to subconscious you meet your client, and feel her pain exactly as she does.

Sadly, this scenario has caused more than one empathically gifted healer to leave the profession in disgrace. Empathy should be respected and developed in healers, not denied. Consider how different the scenario is when the healer understands empathic ability. She senses the emotions of her client and recognizes it as information from her empathic sense. Because she is aware of empathy, she knows what is happening and how she can use the information to her own and her client's benefit. This is a far different scenario than one in which the healer experiences baffling, overwhelming emotions seemingly randomly, outside of her control. You can reclaim control of your reaction to clients and your professional identity when you reconnect with and rebalance your empathic ability.

You may need to acknowledge what underlying beliefs interfere with your ability to protect your empathic sense. Do you expect that you should be the impervious healer, resistant to all painful energies around you? Or are you a very compassionate person who is afraid it is selfish to maintain boundaries between you and the people you help? In reality, you will be the best, most effective professional when you can approach your patients from a grounded center of knowledge and protection. You cannot work with your clients successfully if you are constantly drained by them. It is fairest to your clients and yourself to have healthy boundaries of empathic protection.

It is important to consider the need to balance and protect your empathy while you are at work. Keep a bottle of Yarrow flower essence in your desk. Practice meditating between patients, even if it is just for a few seconds. Allow yourself to have a few moments alone once in a while. This is the hardest change for many healers. Due to your busy work environments, many of you continuously interact with coworkers and patients from the moment you enter the workplace until you leave for home. Take a walk alone for the first five minutes of your lunch break. Close your office door between clients. Use this time to refresh yourself and strengthen your empathic protection.

As an empathic person, you are a gifted healer. You have the innate capacity to understand and communicate with your clients from a truly emotional perspective. In our intellectual world, most patients need this emotional interchange more than anything else.

Working with your empathic sense allows you to connect with your clients in deeper, more beneficial ways than can be achieved intellectually. But remember to also take care of yourself. Working from an empathic perspective requires you to connect with yourself, develop empathic protection, and allow your empathic ability to benefit you as well as your clients.

I hope that you will come to regard your sensitivity from a kinder vantage as I have. It is unfortunate that we have spent most of our lives regarding our sensitivity as a liability. Our empathic sense provides us with advantages at work and in our personal lives when we can listen to what it is telling us without fear, with understanding, and with respect.

Answers to Common Questions

I would like to respond to a few of the most common questions and concerns that mental health professionals have in regard to the alternative theories put forth in this book. I hope these answers will allay your concerns and help you understand how symptoms are viewed from an alternative health perspective.

1. *Why don't you discuss biological and neurochemical theories as other explanations for chronic depression?*

In the biomedical model, psychological symptoms are seen as being the result of biological, neurochemical, or genetic abnormalities. From an alternative health perspective, neurochemical phenomena are seen as signs of imbalance, the physical correlates of the pain that is being expressed emotionally. Biological indicators are not viewed as the actual cause of psychological disorder, nor do they offer a true explanation. They are seen as physical symptoms, just as the distressed emotions and behavior are seen as psychological symptoms. Neurochemical imbalance is the body's response and attempt to adapt to something. But what caused the body to come out of balance? That it what alternative health practitioners seek to find. It is true, of course, that psychotropic medication reduces bothersome symptoms in some cases because it is radically impacting the patient's biochemistry. This does not necessarily mean that the medication has established an explanation of the psychological symptoms; it means that the drug is altering the person's biochemistry, which has its own effects. It is interesting that so many modern day psychologists have become stuck in the physical. Alternative health practitioners seek to go beyond symptoms, to heal the true underlying causes of the patient's emotional and physical imbalance.

2. Aren't sensitive people just people with poor ego strength?

No. Some individuals with low ego strength may be sensitive; and some sensitive people may very well have poor ego strength, but they are not they same. Sensitive people often feel emotionally overwhelmed, but they may not necessarily overtly act overwhelmed. Many sensitive people function very well in their lives. Their struggles are primarily internal. Although they may feel overwhelmed and overcome by emotions, they can pull themselves together to do what they need to do. Individuals with low ego strength, on the other hand, often display their overwhelmed emotions. They cannot cope with stressors, demanding support from others to help them through their crises. Low ego strength is generally thought to be the result of a dysfunctional childhood. The lines blur when an individual is both sensitive and has poor ego strength. The case of Janelle, presented in this book, is an example of such a patient, who might also be called emotionally reactive. In my work I have found that such combination clients can make amazing progress when their sensitivity is addressed, rather than their poor ego strength being the focus of counseling.

3. Aren't you minimizing the obvious causes of depression such as family dysfunction, abuse and trauma?

No. In Chapter Two I list the many causes of depression including abuse. The tone of this book is **not** that empathic ability is the only cause of emotional distress. I convey to readers that empathic ability is a cause that has been overlooked, but that does not exclude all the other sources of emotional pain. My intent is to make people aware of the prevalence of empathic ability, and to encourage people to address their sensitivity, which will in turn allow them to more easily and fully heal their issues such as abuse or trauma.

4. Empathy, the understanding of others' emotional experiences, is well known to psychologists as an important part of any healthy person's personality. Why are you using the word empathy to refer to psychic feeling?

The word *empathy* is prevalent in our language, but its common usage is too shallow. People need to realize that empathy is not the mere intellectual understanding of another's emotions. The history of the word *empathic* refers to the capacity to know another person's emotions without those feelings having been communicated. Empathy and empathic ability have far deeper meanings than their common usage imply. Until people accept that idea and change their usage of the word *empathy* to convey its deeper, psychic meaning, then the word is not being used correctly.

Appendix

Flower Essence Manufacturers & Recommended Remedies

This appendix provides you with contact information for several flower essence makers. Under each brand, I have listed a sampling of their essences that are particularly healing for sensitive, empathic people. I have also listed all the essences that were mentioned in the case examples in Chapter 4.

ALASKAN FLOWER ESSENCE PROJECT
PO Box 1369, Homer, Alaska 99603, phone 1-800-545-9309
www.alaskanessences.com

Grass of Parnassus (*Parnassia palustris*)-Cleanses the aura. Helps you maintain your energy in crowded or toxic environments.

One-Sided Wintergreen (*Pyrola secunda*)-Specifically for those who are strongly influenced by other people's energy. Helps sensitive people become aware of how they are impacted by others. Helps you create energy boundaries, so you can work in close proximity with others without losing your center.

White Violet (*Viola renifolia*)-Helps those who are highly sensitive maintain a strong sense of self and embody their sensitivity in a more comfortable way.

Yarrow (*Achillea borealis*)-This essence is made from white Yarrow flowers. Strengthens the overall integrity of your protective energy field. Helps you know and be the source of your own protection.

Alaskan Essences makes two combination formulas, which I highly recommend:

Guardian-Helps create a powerful energy field of protection around you. Helps you maintain positive, harmonious energies and strong, healthy boundaries.

Purification-Cleanses and purifies your personal energy and your environment.

The descriptions of these essences are from the Alaskan Flower Essence Project 1999 Catalog.

BACH FLOWER ESSENCES
Nelson Bach, USA, Ltd, 100 Research Drive, Wilmington MA 01887, phone 1-800-319-9151
www.nelsonbach.com

Bach remedies were one of the first widely available brands of flower essences. Many Bach essences focus on specific psychological challenges, such as anxiety or depression.

Clematis (*Clematis vitalba*)-Helps people who are at risk of picking up negative energies. Clematis allows you to be more grounded and productive, especially in creative endeavors, such as art, writing and healing.

Mimulus (*Mimulus guttatus*)-Eases anxiety and fear of known things, such as illness, animals, or public speaking. Sensitive people benefit from this essence by learning when and how to withdraw when they need space and time to recharge. It also helps sensitive people be better able to stand up for themselves.

Mustard (*Sinapis arvensis*)-For relief of sudden depression or gloom that descends out of the blue.

Walnut (*Juglans regia*)-A protective essence that helps shield you from outside influences. Useful for therapists or healers who may be feeling drained by their clients. Also used to ease adjustment during times of major life changes.

Descriptions of Bach essences are from *Bach Flower Essences for the Family*, Wigmore Publications, a small, information packed book available from www.nelsonbach.com.

DESERT ALACHEMY FLOWER ESSENCES
PO Box 44189, Tucson, AZ 85733, phone 1-800-736-3382
www.desert-alchemy.com
Desert Marigold-(*Baileya multiradiata*)-Balances solar plexus energy. Helps you regain control over your emotional circumstances.

Jojoba-(*Simmondsia chinensis*)-Helps sensitive people view their sensitive nature as an asset, rather than a liability. It is grounding and provides a sense of security.

Descriptions of these essences are from the Desert Alchemy website.

FEATHERHAWK ESSENCES
PO Box 125, New Albany, Indiana 47151, phone 1-812-949-0478
www.featherhawk.com

Corn-This essence helps you feel more grounded and connected with the earth, and, therefore, less impacted by outside emotions and energies.

Pink Yarrow-Helps you establish firm emotional boundaries.

Sweetgrass-Restores and invigorates your energetic boundaries.

White Yarrow-Boosts your energetic field of protection

Yellow Yarrow-Increases emotional protection and self-confidence.

Featherhawk also makes a **Yarrow Blend**, which boosts overall strengthening of your empathic boundaries.

Descriptions of these essences are from the Featherhawk website.

FES (FLOWER ESSENCE SERVICES)
P.O. Box 1769, Nevada City, CA 95959, phone 1-800-548-0075
www.floweressence.com

Chamomile (*Matricaria recutita*)-Soothes the emotions of those who have very changeable moods. Allows for release of tension from the solar plexus.

Golden Yarrow (*Achillea filipendulina*)-For people who find their sensitivity to be so painful they have reacted by avoiding people or using drugs or alcohol in attempt to blunt their senses.

Lavender (*Lavandula officinalis*)-Soothes high-strung people who are very absorbent of outside energies.

Mimulus (*Mimulus guttatus*)-Helps hypersensitive, anxious people live with more confidence to face life's challenges.

Mountain Pennyroyal (*Monardella odoratissima*)-Helps release negative emotions that feel "stuck" to you. Cleansing and purgative.

Mustard (*Sinapis arvensis*)-Assists the healing process for those who suffer from dark depression or complex depression such as mood swings. Addresses deep, subconscious memories that may be triggering the psychological pain.

Pink Yarrow (*Achillea millefolium var.rubra*)-For those sensitive people who realize they give too much of themselves in relationships. Helps compassionate people who are especially vulnerable to absorbing negative emotions from romantic partners, close friends and family.

Purple Monkeyflower (*Mimulus kelloggii*)-Soothes fear related to experiences of a psychic nature. Resolves the conflict between the person's experience and conventional social-religious expectations.

Yarrow (*Achillea millefolium*)-Specifically helpful for people who are sensitive to their environment and people's thoughts and emotions. Strengthens your energetic boundaries, leaving you more protected from unwanted energy.

Descriptions for FES flower essences are from *Flower Essence Repertory*, published by The Flower Essence Society.

*Remember to follow the manufacturer's directions for the recommended dosage. Each brand may vary slightly in the number of drops per dose.

Glossary

Chronic depression:
Sufferers frequently experience depression (feelings of sadness, gloom, despair, and hopelessness with possible inactivity and suicidal tendencies). They typically experience depressive episodes several times per year.

Emotional sensitivity:
Sensitive people exhibit the following characteristics: They feel emotions deeply, are keenly aware of other people's emotions, are personally affected by emotions they witness, cannot shake off emotions easily, are prone to suffer from emotional distress, and often experience stimulus overload in noisy, hectic environments. These traits of sensitivity are related to the sensitive person's natural empathic ability.

Empathic ability:
The intuitive knowing of another person's emotions or true nature. Empathic ability sometimes manifests as literally feeling another person's emotions as if they were your own feelings.

Flower essence:
An alternative health remedy made from the flowers of various plants. Flower essences are in liquid form and are somewhat similar to homeopathic remedies in that there is little botanical matter in the final

preparation. Flower essences should not be confused with essential oils used in aromatherapy.

Intuition:
Insight and knowledge gained outside of intellectual thought.

Kinesiology:
In the field of alternative health, kinesiology is the practice of using the patient's own muscular responses as an indication of which remedies would work most optimally for him or her. Also called muscle testing.

Meditation:
Focusing one's attention inward, beyond the constant chatter of the mind.

Psychic feeling:
Extrasensory perceptions felt in the form of emotional information. Also known as empathic ability.

Solar plexus:
An interlacing network of nerves located in the abdominal area, which connects to all the internal organs. This is the seat of our "gut feelings," related to empathic ability and psychic feeling.

References

RECOMMENDED BOOKS

Cunningham, Donna. *Flower Remedies Handbook: Emotional Healing & Growth with Bach and Other Flower Essences.* New York: Sterling Publishing Co, 1992.

Johnson, Steve. *The Essence of Healing: A Guide to the Alaskan Flower, Gem, and Environmental Essences.* Homer, AK: Alaskan Flower Essence Project, 1996.

Kaminski, Patricia, and Richard Katz. *Flower Essence Repertory.* Nevada City, CA: Flower Essence Society, 1996.

Sanders, Pete. *You Are Psychic!: The Free Soul Method.* New York: Fireside, 1999.

RECOMMENDED WEBSITES

Dr. Mesich's Website
www.KyraMesich.com

Desert Alchemy Frequently Asked Questions
www.desert-alchemy.com/txt/faq.html#Q1

Flower Essence Research
www.flowersociety.org

Flower Essence Services Frequently Asked Questions
www.floweressence.com/faq.html#ess

Index

About the Author

Kyra Mesich completed her undergraduate studies at the University of South Florida, continuing on to the Florida Institute of Technology where she earned her doctoral degree in clinical psychology from their American Psychological Association approved program. She completed her internship at the Veterans Administration Hospital and the University of Kentucky Hospital in Lexington, Kentucky. In addition to her traditional training, she has studied extensively in the field of alternative health, blending herbalism, flower essence therapy, and energy healing into her current practice. Dr. Mesich works and resides in Minneapolis, Minnesota.

Dr. Mesich welcomes your feedback about this book. You can write to her at: PO Box 80208, Minneapolis, MN 55408.

Please visit Dr. Mesich's website where you can obtain audio files of practice meditations and be kept abreast of her appearances and publications.

www.KyraMesich.com